Enjoy.
Gary F. Brown

Lieutenant Colonel The Rev. FATHER THOMAS NANGLE CF.
Soldier - Priest In the Killing Fields of Europe, WW I.

SOLDIER PRIEST
IN THE KILLING FIELDS OF EUROPE

Padre Thomas Nangle:
Chaplain to the Newfoundland Regiment WWI

by Gary Browne and Darrin McGrath

Library and Archives Canada Cataloguing in Publication

Father Thomas Nangle: soldier-priest in the killing fields of Europe / by Gary Browne and Darrin McGrath.

ISBN 0-9781496-1-0

1. Nangle, Thomas. 2. Great Britain. Army. Royal Newfoundland Regiment--Chaplains--Biography. 3. World War, 1914-1918--Chaplains--Newfoundland and Labrador--Biography.
4. Chaplains, Military--Newfoundland and Labrador--Biography. I. Browne, Gary, 1948- II. Title.

D639.C38M38 2006   940.4'78092   C2006-904862-2

COPYRIGHT ©

ALL RIGHTS RESERVED. No part of this publication may be reproduced stored in a retrieval system or transmitted, in any form or by any means, without the prior written consent of the publisher or a licence form The Canadian Copyright Licensing Agency (Access Copyright).

DRC Publishing

3 Parliament Street
St. John's, NL, A1A 2Y6

Phone 726-0960
E-mail staceypj@nfld.com

Dedication

*This book is dedicated to the memory
of Lieutenant Colonel
The Reverend Father Thomas M. Nangle,
Chaplain to the Forces, and
to the soldiers of the
Royal Newfoundland Regiment
who served in World War One.*

About Padre Nangle

Thomas Nangle died in Rhodesia (now Zimbabwe) on January 4, 1972, at age 83. Known as Tim to family and friends, he was predeceased by his wife, Thelma, and survived by his children: Timothy, Hugh, Rory and Mavourneen. Today, in St. John's, Newfoundland, where he was born and raised, there's a street named in his honour- Padre Nangle Place. Many people, however, may not be aware that the man the street is named after, the man buried next to his wife in a foreign country thousands of miles from his native land was the beloved Roman Catholic chaplain of the Newfoundland Regiment during the First World War.

After the war and while still a priest, Padre Nangle was instrumental in the erection of the National War Memorial in St. John's, the Caribou Memorial Park in Beaumont Hamel, France, and four other similar parks at places in France and Belgium where the Newfoundland Regiment fought and died. In 1926, he left the priesthood and departed Newfoundland, emigrating to Rhodesia where he became a farmer, entered politics, married Thelma Watkinson, and had four children. In the summer of 2006, the Royal Newfoundland Regiment returned in strength to France and Belgium for the first time since the end of the First World War in 1918. They went to remember fallen comrades and rededicate caribou memorials at each of the five parks in France and Belgium. Among those present were three of Nangle's children and retired policeman Gary Browne, chairman of the Royal Newfoundland Regiment Advisory Council and co-author of this book.

EPIGRAPH

"It is good, once in a while, that we should think of the heroes, and heroines too, who have not borne arms. Among the non-combatants who have shown the pluck that is in them, the "padres" have been second to none in their devotion to duty. They have borne 'the ark of the covenant' into the thickest of fighting, and who can deny their valor or value of the aid they brought to the achievement of success? In season and out of season, in the rest camps or on the blood stained battlefield, they were ever present, encouraging, admonishing and comforting.

When the nurses and doctors had given up of saving the life of the victim of war, the chaplain persisted to the last in the fight to save the soul. It was his privilege to take the place of the father and mother, sister and wife, son and daughter at the death bed of their loved ones. Amid the roar of the guns and bursting shells and surrounded by the hideous din of war, the messengers of the Prince of Peace calmly performed their duty. It was to them that the last messages for their loved ones were given by the dying soldiers, and it was from them they received the spiritual food for their journey for the last long trail. Among those who so ardently pressed their claims was the subject of this article, the Reverend Captain Thomas Nangle. He has been to the very gates of hell on earth which we call war. He has been in the thick of it, often, as Governor Davidson put it, "repeatedly working under fire, regardless of the instructions that he should keep out of it." Of such stuff, Nangle was made. The broad minded spirit of the man raised him above petty sectarianism and he bestowed praise alike on men of all denominations. All in his eyes were true crusaders, or, as that word means, Soldiers of The Cross. Thank God, there were such men as he, to light into the Dark Valley of the Shadow of Death so many of those of our brave boys who will never return to their homeland, and to give them opportunity to fasten their dying gaze on the symbol of man's redemption. To him and others who bore no arms but who are none the less heroes, all praise is do. They too fight the good fight and helped others to win victories over even more bestial enemies than the cruel, treacherous Hun."

Source: The Newfoundland Magazine, March 1919
(author unknown)

Table of Contents

Foreword by His Honour Edward Roberts, Lieutenant Governor of Newfoundland and Labrador

Preface by Gary Browne

Authors' Acknowledgments

Chapter One	- Introduction	1
Chapter Two	- Early Years	4
Chapter Three	- Start of World War One	9
Chapter Four	- Gallipoli	16
Chapter Five	- July 1, 1916	20
Chapter Six	- The War Continues	32
Chapter Seven	- Recruiting	59
Chapter Eight	- Wounded	65
Chapter Nine	- War Graves Commission	70
Chapter Ten	- Caribou Memorials	82
Chapter Eleven	- Planning the Memorials	88
Chapter Twelve	- Newfoundland's War Memorial	95
Chapter Thirteen	- Fund-raising	101
Chapter Fourteen	- Cochius' Vision	109
Chapter Fifteen	- Building a National Memorial	113
Chapter Sixteen	- Unveiling	118
Chapter Seventeen	- Trail of the Caribou Completed	127
Chapter Eighteen	- Leaving the Priesthood	132
Chapter Nineteen	- Conclusion	141
Photo Sections		39 - 58, 139 - 140
Appendice		149
References		163

Foreword

by **His Honour Edward Roberts**
Lieutenant Governor of Newfoundland and Labrador

Thomas Nangle was a remarkable man who made a remarkable contribution to Newfoundland. His achievements were widely recognized and much praised in the years after the Great War of 1914-18, but have never been properly acknowledged in the historical record. Gary Browne and Darrin McGrath set out to right this wrong. They have done so by writing a very fine biography of him.

SOLDIER - PRIEST IN THE KILLING FIELDS OF EUROPE, WW I:

The 1st Newfoundland Regiment was Newfoundland's major contribution to the Great War. (King George V honoured it with the title of "Royal" early in 1918, the only Regiment so honoured during the war). Its story is one of mingled pride and grief. The gallantry and courage of our Regiment is an indelible part of our heritage. More than 12,000 Newfoundlanders came forward to join it: 6,200 actually wore the caribou badge - its emblem. One in five of those men lost their lives in the war. The Regiment's Colours still proudly bear the Battle Honours won by those young Newfoundlanders at Gallipoli, on the Somme and elsewhere on the Western Front. Their comrades lie buried in a score of cemeteries on those same battlefields.

The Battle of Beaumont Hamel on 1 July 1916 is known to every Newfoundlander and Labradorian. Nearly 800 officers and men of the Regiment attacked that morning, as part of the British army's assault on the first day of the Battle of the Somme. The engagement lasted for only a few short minutes: it was all over in less than a half hour. Nine out of ten of the Newfoundlanders became casualties: 272 were killed or died of their wounds. The Regiment did not suffer alone: 57,000 British soldiers were killed or wounded that day. A half-million more became casualties during the remaining months of the Somme Battle.

Nangle, a Roman Catholic priest, was the Regiment's first padre, serving until the very end of the war. He was a friend to every soldier, comforting them against their physical afflictions and providing them with spiritual guidance, and often at great risk to himself. But his most sterling service to those who wore the caribou badge came after the war. In the years that followed the Armistice, he did more than any other Newfoundlander to honour those who had fought, and particularly those who died.

At war's end, Father Nangle volunteered to help to ensure that the Newfoundlanders killed in the conflict had proper resting places. He was appointed to the Imperial War Graves Commission (now the Commonwealth War Graves Commission) as the Dominion's representative. For the next six years he laboured to find the bodies of his fellow Newfoundlanders, to identify them, and to ensure that they were interred with reverence and dignity.

Many consider this his greatest contribution. But it was not the only one.

Five majestic caribou memorials stand today on the Western Front battlefields where the Regiment fought. A sixth stands in St. John's, in Bowring Park. Each is an enduring tribute to the men who took part in those battles. And each is also an enduring memorial to Tom Nangle, the man who conceived the noble notion that the caribou should be the centrepiece of each battlefield's commemoration of the 1914-18 Regiment. He did much, too, to bring about Newfoundland's National War Memorial, which stands in St. John's looking over the harbour and through the Narrows. Together, these magnificent monuments pay fitting honour to those who served King and country.

The story of Tom Nangle disappeared from our ken, in large measure because he left the priesthood. He moved to Rhodesia, where he made his home for the rest of his life. The authors have delved deeply into the Regimental records and other archival holdings, and unearthed much new information about the man and his achievements. The book is an accurate, complete and enthralling account of the life's work of one who served his fellow Newfoundlanders well.

All who are interested in the story of the Royal Newfoundland Regiment and the men who served under its Colours will enjoy this book, and learn much from it. As the Regiment's Honorary Colonel and as Lieutenant Governor of Newfoundland and Labrador, I commend Mr. Browne and Mr. McGrath. They have written a fitting tribute to a man who deserves to be remembered. He truly was one of those who were "better than the best."

Preface
by Gary Browne

2006 France/Flanders Pilgrimage Concludes

It is 9 a.m. on July 3, 2006 as I join my wife and daughter at the kitchen table for breakfast following seven days filled with emotion, grueling high temperatures and an exceptionally aggressive itinerary in France and Belgium. I had accompanied the Royal Newfoundland Regiment on a pilgrimage of remembrance, commemoration, and rededication of memorial parks to mark the 90th Anniversary of the Battle of The Somme, World War One (WW1). It was the first time that the full regiment (Band, 1st and 2nd Battalions) had been back in Europe since the end of the war in 1918.

My wife asks me to tell all about my trip to Europe, and at that moment I was engulfed in a wave of emotion that was difficult to control. The impact of retracing "The Trail of The Caribou" to the five Newfoundland WW1 memorials sites in France and Belgium, and visiting numerous military graveyards with many thousands of white crosses had finally caught up with me.

This groundswell of emotions began some eight months ago when I decided to co-author a book on Lieutenant Colonel Thomas Nangle who had been the Roman Catholic padre for the [Royal] Newfoundland Regiment in France and Flanders during WW1. For countless long days in archival institutions, and on the World Wide Web we pondered over hundreds of photographs, personal letters, military, government and church documents in an earnest attempt to give credit to a man who was all but forgotten by history. I had, in the last seven days in Europe stood on the very soil where our regiment won glory, was decimated and where it lost so many proud and brave Newfoundlanders. Could these experiences now be the reason for the over flowing of my emotional rain-barrel?

On June 27, a hot summer's day, we stood in a farmer's field just outside of the small French village of Gueudecourt in the Newfoundland Memorial Park which was dedicated to the men of the regiment who fought and died there 90 years ago. As I gazed upon the life-sized statue of our native Newfoundland caribou, whose impressive and defiant figure looked out towards the German lines of WW1, my mind wandered back to this very place when the horrendous sounds of war permeated the air. Suddenly I was jolted back to the present by the loud order of the regiment's commanding officer - "By the left quick march"- as they smartly stepped off, and as the band struck up "The Banks of Newfoundland." During the commemoration and rededication ceremony the padre of the regiment, The Rev. Capt. Shawn Samson, and a local clergyman blessed the monument and the adjacent fields where the remains of unknown soldiers still lie, forever young beneath the French soil. Yet again my mind's-eye creates a vision of another youthful padre blessing the dying soldiers as our regiment fought its way across the Western Front during WW1.

With the completion of the ceremony at the Memorial Park, I took my place behind the regiment and we marched off down a very narrow country road towards the village of Gueudecourt as the band played more Newfoundland music. As we marched passed the very fields where our soldiers fought and died I could envisage their youthful spirits shouting out to us, "Now by's, throw out those chests and carry your heads high, because you are the Royal Newfoundland Regiment, and you represent us." As we approached the town square we were met by the cheers of young children and adults waving Newfoundland, Canadian and French flags. It was as if history was repeating itself.

Similar scenes of cheering crowds would be played out at the other memorial sites of Monchy-le-Preux, Beaumont Hamel, Masnieres in France, and Courtrai(Kortrijk) in Belgium.

Then there were the unforgettable memories of meeting three of Padre Nangle's children and other family members and their spouses at Monchy and at Beaumont Hamel; participating in the very moving sunset ceremony and laying a wreath at the Menin Gate; standing at the Caribou Memorial in Beaumont Hamel with Miller Ayre of St. John's, who lost four of his family in battle on July 1,1916; walking through the trenches and the cemetery at Beaumont Hamel with Padre Ian Wishart; standing by the grave of Lieutenant Walter Greene of Cape Broyle (a Newfoundland Constabulary officer killed in WW1) with three other Constabulary officers from today's regiment; personally laying a wreath at the foot of the caribou at Beaumont Hamel on July 1, being present at Monchy-le-Preux for the emotionally charged address of Edward Roberts, the Regiment's Honourary Colonel and Lieutenant Governor of Newfoundland and Labrador; listening to the many very fine historical reviews given by renown regimental historian, Dr. David Parsons, as we moved from site to site to name just a few of my remarkable experiences.

I will forever remember the stirring and patriotic Newfoundland march music played by our renowned Royal Newfoundland Band, under the very capable direction of Captain John Powell CD., as we proudly marched through the streets of France and Belgium.I must also express the tremendous pride, as a Newfoundlander and Labradorian, I had in the men and women of the Royal Newfoundland Regiment, and their military support staff who went to France and Belgium on the pilgrimage. Their pride of unit, people and of place was nothing short of spectacular, and their parade professionalism was second to none. Newfoundland and Labrador, and Canada, can rest assured that the regiment is alive, well and vibrant as it adds to its illustrious military history of being "Better Than The Best."

Personally, it was very gratifying to make the pilgrimage to France and Flanders along with my friends and colleagues of our very active regimental advisory council; "The Newfoundland"

Friends of The Regiment"; handpicked young Army cadets from our province; and members of the Veterans Affairs Canada contingent which included the Minister of Veterans Affairs Gregory F. Thompson, Minister of Fisheries Loyola Hearn, Premier of Newfoundland and Labrador Danny Williams, Member of Parliament for the Newfoundland constituency of Avalon Fabian Manning, veterans, members of the Royal Canadian Legion, Canadian youth representatives, ceremonial guard members of the Royal Newfoundland Constabulary and the Royal Canadian Mounted Police, and a score of other important people.

It would be remiss of me if I did not highly praise the Commonwealth War Graves Commission and the Canadian Department of Veterans Affairs for the superb job they do in their stewardship role of maintaining and upgrading the grave and memorial sites in France and Belgium. Veterans Affairs Canada's "Canadian Battlefield Memorials Restoration Project" now nearing completion is worthy of much praise for the repairing, restoring and rehabilitation of Canadian memorial sites. The restoration includes work on each of the 13 WW1 memorial sites in France and Belgium (8 established by Canada and 5 established by Newfoundland).Accolades should also be given to Parks Canada and their dedicated professional staff for the daily administration and interpretation of these magnificent memorial sites.

"The Trail of The Caribou" is completed for me now, and it has left an emotional imprint that I will never forget. I only hope that this book will do some justice to the memory of Padre Thomas Nangle, and to the men of the Royal Newfoundland Regiment who fought, and those who died for the cause of freedom so many years ago in Gallipoli and in Europe during WWI.

Acknowledgements

First and foremost, the authors wish to thank their respective wives, Paula Browne and Ann McGrath, for their unwavering love, support and encouragement during all phases of this project. Their patience made writing this book so much easier. Gary Browne also wants to acknowledge the support of his children: Chris, Greg and Danielle.

Thanks to the children of Tom Nangle: Timothy, Hugh, Rory and Mavourneen for their support of this project. A special thanks to Hugh for sharing loving memories of his father.

The authors owe a debt of gratitude to Lieutenant Governor Edward Roberts, Honorary Colonel of the Royal Newfoundland Regiment, for agreeing to write the forward to the book. His assistance and encouragement was greatly appreciated.

Similarly, the authors are grateful for the support of Lieutenant Colonel Sean Leonard, the Commanding Officer of the First Battalion, Royal Newfoundland Regiment.

Archbishop Brendan O'Brien of the Roman Catholic Archdiocese of St. John's who was most interested in this project. Thanks to Larry Dohey at the Roman Catholic Archives of the Archdiocese of St. John's and to Sandra Ronayne, Cal Best, Melanie Tucker, Greg Walsh, Manny Bucheit and other staff at the Provincial Archives. Thank you to Brother J.B. Darcy who assisted with the records of St. Bon's College; Neachel Keeping and Helen Miller at the City of St. John's Archives and the staff at the Centre for Newfoundland Studies, Memorial University, and special thanks to Deborah Andrews and Mrs. Weir. The employees of the A.C. Hunter Library, Newfoundland Room were a great asset as well, special thanks to Dr. Thomas Nemec.

Patrick O'Flaherty, Shannon Ryan, Andrea Rose, Dr. John Fitzgerald, William R. Callahan and Lisa Moore furthered the project by lending necessary references. Dr. Tom Cantwell was extremely helpful in explaining post-traumatic stress disorder and survivor's guilt. Others who assisted us include: John Greene; Father V. Boyd, Principal of St. Bonaventure's College; Mr. Aiden Maloney; Dave Barker; Dr. David Parsons; Arlene King; and Steve Austin of Veteran's Affairs Canada; Paul O'Neill; Elizabeth and Phil Lewis; Mrs. Margaret (Greene) O'Brien; Mrs. Bernice (Greene) Blake. LCol. Aubrey Halfyard, Chair of RNR Museum Committee, Major Jim Lynch CD., Mr. Charlie Greene, Mr. John Fleet, John O'Mara and A.J. St. Croix.

Many thanks to Peter and Jean Stacey of DRC Publishing. A tip of the hat to Diane Lynch for cover design and layout. Thank you to The Downhome magazine which ran an excerpt from the book in the July 2006 issue.

Special thanks to Cindy (Ball) Fleet, formerly of Grand Falls and daughter of Catherine Ball, for making available photographs from her mother's album of her beloved uncle, Captain Gerald J. Whitty, O.B.E., M.C. of the Royal Newfoundland Regiment 1914-1918, and secretary of the Great War Veterans Association. The Whitty album provided numerous outstanding historical pictures, some never publically seen before, with captions related to the Regiment.

Gary Browne and Darrin McGrath
St. John's, Newfoundland, 2006

Caribou - Beaumont Hamel Park, France

~ Chapter One ~

INTRODUCTION

Thomas Matthew Mary Nangle was born in St. John's, Newfoundland, in 1889 and educated at St. Bonaventure's College. He attended the seminary in Ireland, All Hallows, Dublin, and St. Patrick's College in Carlow, and was ordained a priest at the Roman Catholic Basilica of St. John the Baptist in St. John's in 1913.

In July 1916, he enlisted in the Newfoundland Regiment and went overseas where he became part of the Royal Army Chaplain's Department. He was subsequently attached to the 88th Brigade Field Ambulance, British Expeditionary Force and in October of 1916 was appointed chaplain to the First Battalion, Newfoundland Regiment.

As chaplain of the Regiment in the Great War, he played a major role working in the trenches, burying the dead, consoling the wounded, comforting families and motivating the troops. Padre Nangle received a wound to his shoulder on April 24, 1917.

Former Premier Joseph R. Smallwood described Nangle as popular with all the troops in the Regiment regardless of denomination.

After the cessation of hostilities, Padre Nangle was appointed Director of War Graves, Registration, Enquiries and Memorials, and was further appointed by Newfoundland Prime Minister Sir Richard Squires as Newfoundland's representative to the Imperial War Graves Commission of Britain.

As Director of War Graves, he personally supervised the exhumation of known graves, the construction of Newfoundland's 15 war graveyards in Europe and Gallipoli, the building of five caribou memorials (4 in France, 1 in Belgium) and the construction and unveiling of the National War Memorial in St. John's at King's Beach.

In 1926, after reaching all of his personal goals in relation to the Newfoundland graveyards and memorials, and after leaving the priesthood, he emigrated to Rhodesia, South Africa, where he became a farmer, entered politics and married Thelma Watkinson. The couple had four children: Timothy, Hugh, Rory and Mavourneen.

Social Relevance

This book on Thomas Nangle has many socially relevant features. It is the firm belief of the authors that Nangle has been essentially all but forgotten and neglected in Newfoundland history. He is, for example, completely omitted from the Dictionary of Newfoundland and Labrador Biography (1990). It is the opinion of Aiden Maloney, a former Member of the House of Assembly and Minister of the Crown, that the authors of this book are writing about a "major Newfoundland historical oversight, namely Thomas Nangle."

Also socially relevant is the fact that 2006 marks the ninetieth anniversary of the Battle of the Somme, July 1, 1916 - November 18, 1916. A part of this major British offensive was the infamous Battle of Beaumont Hamel, a defining moment in Newfoundland history, at which the Newfoundland Regiment was almost wiped out. After the war, Nangle played a lead role and was the major driving force in the construction of the

Caribou Memorial Park at Beaumont Hamel, France. He contracted both the sculptor of the caribou, Captain Basil Gotto, and famous landscape architect Rudolph Cochius. Padre Nangle was authorized by Newfoundland Prime Minister Sir Richard Squires to negotiate with 250 French landowners and acquire the land needed to establish Beaumont Hamel Memorial Park. He also played a lead role in the creation of the four other caribou memorials in France and Belgium.

At war's end, Nangle was responsible for exhuming Newfoundland's scattered war dead, identifying the remains and gathering them into proper military cemeteries. He was the Regiment's link with the families of the fallen, writing to loved ones and sending home pictures of grave markers.

He also played a major role in the construction of the National War Memorial on Water Street in St. John's, and was Aide-de-Camp to British Field Marshal Sir Earl Haig when he unveiled the memorial on July 1, 1924.

Yet another socially relevant feature of this book is that one of the co-authors of this project, Gary F. Browne, is the chairperson of the Royal Newfoundland Regiment Advisory Council. One of the chief mandates of the council is to identify, preserve and herald historical items of note concerning the Regiment. This year, for the first time since 1918, the Royal Newfoundland Regiment returned in strength to Beaumont Hamel for the solemn ceremony on July 1 and the rededication of the five Caribou Memorials. Her Royal Highness The Princess Royal, Colonel-in-Chief of the Regiment, was also in Beaumont Hamel on June 30 and July 1.

Finally, the telling of Nangle's story will hopefully satisfy his family who wonder why their father's contribution to the war effort has been overlooked in Newfoundland. This book was made all the richer with the assistance of Tom Nangle's son, Hugh, who patiently answered numerous questions, and shared personal memories of his father and family.

~ CHAPTER TWO ~

EARLY YEARS

Thomas Matthew Mary Nangle was born in St. John's, Newfoundland, on an Indian Summer's day on September 5, 1889. He was the first child of Thomas and Mary Ellen (Kelly) Nangle. His parents, who were married on August 21, 1887 by Reverend Father J. Ryan, were elated with the birth of a son and proudly named him after his father. Matthew, the infant's middle name, came from his father's brother, and Mary from his mother and also the Mother of God. Putting the name Mary on a male child was fairly common in the Roman Catholic religion at the time and exemplified his parents' deep felt faith. Young Thomas would be brought up with this strong, Irish-based faith and it would influence his life.

On August 5th, 1583 Sir Humphrey Gilbert landed on King's Beach, St. John's, and claimed Newfoundland for England's Queen Elizabeth. Over the years, St. John's harbour proved to be a safe haven for vessels from all over the world. It was in this venerable city that Thomas Nangle developed a strong sense of pride of people and place which would follow him for the rest of his life. He was born and raised on Queen's Road in downtown St. John's, an area of hilly streets and wooden row houses covered in painted clapboard. Like Humphrey Gilbert, Nangle would eventually make his own mark on King's Beach.

He grew up listening to the distinctive accents of emigrants from the West Country of England or the strong Irish brogues from Wexford, Waterford, or County Cork. The massive stone

Roman Catholic Basilica stands on a hill looking down over this section of St. John's. At the foot of the hill the nearby harbour smacks of salt-water and ever present winds baffle and blow, carrying thick fog throughout the seasons of the year.

Tom's father was a tailor by trade and owned a clothing shop on Duckworth Street. His Uncle Matthew ran a grocery store, also located on Duckworth Street.

Thomas senior did not live to see his namesake grow to manhood. Young Tom was less than a year old when his father passed away on January 24, 1890. Ellen later remarried a St. John's man named Patrick Murphy, a West End Road Inspector and owner of many St. John's properties, including Murphy's Range on LeMarchant Road.

In the late 1880's there was a fairly large extended family of Nangles living in St. John's. Today, the family name "Nangle" is not found in the city's telephone directory, but there are distant cousins still living in the Metro area.

Early Schooling

Ellen enrolled Tom in St. Bonaventure's (St. Bon's) College on August 30, 1896. He was No. 396 on the school register. The school dates from 1857, when it was started by Bishop Thomas Mullock as a seminary-cum-academy for the Roman Catholic boys of Newfoundland. In 1889, the seminary was almost bankrupt and the Irish Christian Brothers took full responsibility for the school. So when Tom Nangle started school in 1896 it was at an institution run by Irish Brothers, a setting in which education and faith were woven together.

Initially, Tom started out as "a day boy," a student who attended classes during the day and returned home in the evening. But St. Bon's also had students who boarded in the massive stone dormitory attached to the school on Bonaventure Avenue. Tom began boarding at the school in September of 1904 when he was 15.

He was an average student and a superior athlete (see photo section). He excelled in track and field sports such as high jump, hurdles and pole vault and was on St. Bon's football, cricket and ice hockey teams. As well, he was an altar boy and was involved in theatre. In 1908 he starred in the play "Triumph of Justice."

He was also a member of the Catholic Cadet Corps (CCC). The CCC was founded in 1896, according to archivist Larry Dohey, and had five companies in St. John's - the West End and East End Companies, plus school companies at St. Bonaventure's, St. Patrick's, and Holy Cross.

Tom wrote his preliminary exam in 1905, followed by his intermediate (equivalent to high school) the following year. However, despite having completed his formal studies in 1906, he remained at St. Bon's until June 30, 1909 at which time he entered the seminary in Ireland to study for the priesthood. Archivist and Christian Brother J.B. Darcy says it was not unusual for boarders intending to enter the priesthood to stay at St. Bon's before leaving for the seminary. The fact that Tom was a great athlete ensured his acceptance in St. Bon's, a school where athletics and scholarship ran neck and neck in status.

The Seminary

Tom began his ecclesiastical studies for the priesthood at All Hallow's College in Dublin, Ireland in 1909, according to the records of the Roman Catholic Archdiocese.

He remained at All Hallow's for two years at which time he transferred to St. Patrick's College Seminary in Carlow, Ireland.

He spent a further two years at St. Patrick's. On July 18, 1912 John Foley, one of the administrators of the college, wrote to Newfoundland Archbishop Michael Howley advising him of Nangle's progress:

> *Mr. Nangle is doing well. He is a nice student, his manners are good, his abilities are fair. He has made progress in theology although he is not proficient in speaking Latin...which is a drawback in theology classes since Latin is the instrument used to convey theological knowledge...I am hoping he will make a useful Priest when the time comes.*

On May 9, 1913 Foley wrote the archbishop and informed him that Nangle had been ordained a sub-deacon and required approximately two more years training for the priesthood.

Foley's letter was preceded by a correspondence Nangle sent Archbishop Howley on May 6th saying that St. Patrick's College had refused to admit him to the exams for the priesthood and he was leaving on the next vessel for St. John's.

On May 17, 1913 Foley again wrote the Archbishop and intimated that the seminary administration felt that Nangle needed more forming for the priesthood. In this letter Foley acknowledged that Howley was very badly in need of priests in St John's.

Not only was Archbishop Howley in need of priests, he was also in the process of "Newfoundlandizing" the Roman Catholic church. Born in St. John's in 1843 and ordained in 1868, Howley became archbishop of St. John's in 1904. In previous years, priests who served in Newfoundland almost all came from Ireland. As the first Newfoundland-born Archbishop, Howley was concerned with ordaining more Newfoundlanders to the priesthood. Despite resistance from St. Patrick's College in Ireland he forged ahead with his commitment to ordain more native-born priests. Upon Tom Nangle's return to St.

John's, Howley ordained him a Roman Catholic priest on June 29, 1913. The ordination at the Cathedral of St. John the Baptist was reported by *the Daily News*:

> *His Grace the Archbishop conferred the dignity of the Priesthood on the Rev. Thomas Nangle yesterday at Last Mass. The beautiful and solemn ceremonial of the Roman Pontifical was carried out in a perfect manner. His Grace was assisted by Revs. Fr. McDermott and Dr. Greene. Present also in the sanctuary were Rev. Dr. Kitchen, Frs. Sheehan, O'Callaghan and Pippy.*

After his ordination, Reverend Father Nangle took up his priestly ministry in St. Thomas of Villa Nova parish, Topsail. From there he served at the Cathedral of St. John the Baptist parish in St. John's, and at St. Michael's parish on Bell Island. Seventy-five year-old Howard Dyer of St. John's, originally from Bell Island, says his parents, William Dyer and Bridget Hyde of Red Head Cove, Bay de Verde, were married by Father Nangle on February 16, 1916. "I can remember Mom saying what a fine looking man Father Nangle was, and that he later served in the war, and was well liked by the troops," Mr. Dyer fondly recalls.

After leaving Bell Island, Father Nangle served from 1914 - 1916 at St. Patrick's parish, in Riverhead, St. John's. This was to be his last parish before the drums of war called him overseas to the Newfoundland Regiment.

~ CHAPTER THREE ~

START OF WORLD WAR ONE

In the summer of 1914 Newfoundland was a country at peace. Fishing schooners came and went from her shores, and Newfoundland salt fish was a much sought commodity the world over. Newfoundland was a colony of Great Britain and war was the last thing on anyone's mind. But on August 4, a message from the Secretary of State for the Colonies was received by the Governor in St. John's. The message stated simply that war had broken out between Great Britain and Germany. The declaration of war followed Germany's invasion of Belgium.

On August 21, 1914 a proclamation was issued in Newfoundland asking for men to serve overseas in the First Newfoundland Regiment. In early September the Newfoundland Legislature's General Assembly enacted "AN ACT RESPECTING A VOLUNTEER FORCE IN THIS COLONY."

At the time war was declared, Newfoundland had very limited military resources and structures. As noted by author Richard Cramm in his book *The First Five Hundred*, "from a military standpoint no country could be in a state of greater unpreparedness" than Newfoundland. Some of the few organizations in which young men had gained some military experience were the four church-sponsored, St. John's-based boys' cadet brigades, the Church Lads Brigade (CLB-Church of England); the Newfoundland Highlanders (Presbyterian); the

Methodist Guards Brigade and the Catholic Cadet Corp (CCC). All of these groups provided many of the early enlistments for the Newfoundland Regiment.

The night the Newfoundland Regiment held its first recruitment meeting, forty members of the CCC marched in a body to the CLB Armoury on Harvey Road in St. John's and enlisted. They were followed by 160 other members of the Corps. Twenty-four members of the Bell Island company also volunteered.

By October, the Newfoundland Regiment had 537 volunteers under canvas at Pleasantville in St. John's. They were known as "The First Five Hundred". They were also called "Blue Puttees" because, lacking khaki material for puttees (strips of cloth which wrapped around the leg from knee to ankle), they ended up with puttees of navy blue, made of material supplied by the CLB.

By October 4th, less than two months after the initial call for recruits, The First Five Hundred volunteers sailed from St. John's on the S.S. Florizel. During the time they were in camp at Pleasantville, the Catholic members of the Blue Puttees had two chaplains to look after their spiritual needs, Rev. Dr. John Carter and Father Jeremiah Conway. But no Catholic chaplain, or chaplain of any denomination, sailed overseas with the Regiment. However, Regimental No. 415 Private R.W. Stenlake was a Methodist student who led prayer services, and once the Regiment went into action at Gallipoli acted as a "padre substitute" to pray over the wounded and bury the dead.

Private Francis "Mayo" Lind of the Newfoundland Regiment wrote a series of letters about life on the Front which were featured in *The Daily News*. In one dated September 27, 1915 he mentioned "Brother Stenlake" and his idea that "shells and bullets are of course rather awkward to have dropping about you, but having a word of prayer, even in the jaws of death, is more important."

According to military historian James Hagerty, there were only 17 Roman Catholic chaplains with the British Army's Chaplains Department in 1914. There were also 89 Church of England and 11 Presbyterian padres. Hagerty says only seven Catholic chaplains accompanied the British Expeditionary Force to France in 1914, and by October another five had been added. Clearly, at the outbreak of the war, having a chaplain alongside the troops was not a major priority for the British Army.

On October 15, 1914, a few days after the Florizel's sailing, Archbishop Howley died in St. John's. With his passing, Father Tom Nangle lost a friend, mentor and colleague.

Edward Patrick Roche succeeded Howley as Archbishop of St. John's and at forty years of age became the youngest Catholic archbishop in the Empire. Coincidentally, at about the same time the Roman Catholic church in Newfoundland underwent a leadership change, the worldwide Roman Catholic church ushered in a new era. Pope Pius X died August 14, 1914, and was replaced by Benedict XV.

On arrival in England, the Newfoundland Regiment was sent to Salisbury Plain for seven weeks training. They followed up with ten months of training in Scotland, at places that included Fort George near Inverness and Stobs Camp near Hawick and Edinburgh Castle.

On December 1, 1914 Father Nangle wrote to Sir Walter Davidson, Newfoundland's Governor from 1913-1917 and also Commanding Officer of the Newfoundland Regiment, asking to be appointed chaplain of the second contingent of fighting Newfoundlanders going overseas:

Dear Sir:
Were it not for the fact that clerics are not permitted to "carry arms" (except in those countries where conscription is

the law of the land) I would have applied for a commission as Captain in our first contingent. But now that you are sending a second contingent I think the number of my co-religionists would warrant the appointment of a Chaplain. This would increase your expenses by about $4.00 per day, or $1,460.00 per year. I therefore have a proposition to make.

The first contingent is over-officered. You have men serving below their rank. At the same time for the purposes of training you will want the full complement of officers for your second contingent. I therefore apply for a commission as Chaplain acting captain....This will mean a saving to your "war chest", an incentive to my fellow Catholics to come forward, and will take away the objection many parents have to their sons enlisting. If necessary I am ready to go on a recruiting campaign in our Catholic districts where I am sure I could secure squads.

I have applied to England and to Canada for a commission but their countries have many applications from their own men. Hoping that you and your committee will be able to grant my request.

> *I remain,*
> *Yours faithfully,*
> *Thos. Nangle*

Nangle wanted to serve his King and Country alongside his schoolmates, friends, parishioners and fellow Newfoundlanders. He was no doubt influenced by his background in the Catholic Cadet Corps and the fact that many of his CCC comrades had joined the Regiment. On New Year's Day 1915, the Newfoundland Regiment suffered its first loss when 20-year-old Private John Chaplin, one of the First Five Hundred and a former student of St. Bonaventure's College and member of the CCC, passed away suddenly from an abdominal condition at Fort George, Scotland. He was given a full military funeral and his remains interred at Ardersier parish churchyard in Scotland.

On January 19, 1915, Governor Davidson wrote to Archbishop E.P. Roche regarding the necessity of assigning a Roman Catholic chaplain to the Newfoundland Regiment.

The next day, a letter came from the Palace (the archbishop's residence) to the governor stating that the Patriotic Association had not requested a chaplain, and for that they were grateful, because they were rather short of priests at present and could ill afford to spare even one.

The Newfoundland Patriotic Association was a non-partisan body of citizens numbering 300 island-wide. Its initial purpose was to raise and equip a military force of 500 plus reserves. Its responsibilities grew to encompass most aspects of the war effort.

For a time, Father Tom Nangle's persistent efforts to join the troops in Europe, as a chaplain, were stalled.

However, while Roche was short of priests, he was at the same time concerned about the spiritual needs of Newfoundland's Roman Catholic soldiers. On January 26, 1915 he wrote to the Archbishop of Westminister and stated:

> *Naturally the parents and other relatives and friends of the Catholic soldiers will be looking to me for information as to what provision is being made in England for their spiritual welfare.*

In February, the British auxiliary cruiser *HMS Clan MacNaughton* was sunk and twenty-two Newfoundland naval reservists in her crew were lost. It was suspected the ship had struck a mine or was torpedoed. The following month, according to historian Patrick O'Flaherty, the *HMS Bayano* was torpedoed near the British Isles and eleven Newfoundlanders in her crew were lost.

In April 1915, Private Peter Cashin (a future politician of note) and more than 250 members of "F" Company of the Newfoundland Regiment left St. John's on the *Calgarian* to serve as reinforcements in Companies "A, B, C and D" of The First Five Hundred. "Many of those...fine young Newfoundlanders were destined to never see Newfoundland again," Cashin later wrote in his memoirs. He and Nangle were about the same age and both had attended St. Bon's. They likely knew each other and seeing Cashin sailing off to war would have fueled Nangle's desire to get to the Front. By this time, the total land force overseas was 1,250 Newfoundlanders.

On August 16, 1915, Newfoundland Governor Davidson received correspondence from the Roman Catholic Palace concerning the appointment of a Catholic chaplain for the Regiment. By then, the church hierarchy had changed its stance on the need for a chaplain:

> *Conditions with regard to the regiment have changed very considerably since the question of a Chaplain was discussed here last year. At that time, as you remember, I did not make any effort to have a Chaplain appointed as I was given to understand by the Head of the Roman Catholics Chaplain's Department at Westminister that our men would be well looked after. Owing, however, to the vast increase in the army since that time, I think that the Chaplains have not been able to attend to the wants of all the men. Representations have been made to me that our men would be distinctly the better for the presence of a Chaplain amongst them, so I am writing to know whether anything has been done towards having one of our Priests appointed....I have come to the conclusion that, both for the sake of our men themselves, and for the sake of their friends here, the appointment of a Chaplain would be desirable. At the same time, I do not wish to do anything that might create an embarrassing situation for your Excellency personally, or for the Committee.*

On August 17, 1915, the Newfoundland Regiment overseas was informed they would be sent to the Front. Three days later, the Newfoundlanders boarded the transport ship *Megantic* enroute to Suvla Bay on the Gallipoli Peninsula.

To make clear his desire to have a Roman Catholic chaplain appointed to the Regiment, Archbishop Roche again wrote the Governor on August 20th stating, "I may say that I am in a position to nominate a chaplain for military service."

So it seems that the Roman Catholic church hierarchy in St. John's had changed its mind on the need for a chaplain at a time when there was a serious shortage of priests at home. However, this does not imply that Father Nangle's request to be appointed chaplain was forthcoming. In fact, it appeared that he was to be overlooked for the chaplain's role. That is, until he took drastic measures.

~ Chapter Four ~
GALLIPOLI

In 1915, with armies on the Western Front bogged down in trench warfare, Winston Churchill, Britain's First Lord of the Admiralty, proposed an attack intended to knock Turkey out of the war and strengthen Russia's efforts on the Eastern Front. Allied troops landed at Cape Helles on the tip of the Gallipoli Peninsula on April 25. The Allies, however, made no headway against the entrenched Turks and a period of trench warfare began.

Members of the Newfoundland Regiment arrived in Suvla Bay on September 19, 1915. The following day the Newfoundlanders went ashore on Kangaroo Beach and were shelled for the first time by the enemy. Heavy shelling from Turkish batteries resulted in one officer and eight men wounded that first day, says historian Richard Cramm. The Newfoundland Regiment had its first fatal casualty in action at Suvla Bay. Private Hugh McWhirter, age 21, who was hit by a Turkish shell on September 22, 1915, is buried in Hill 10 Cemetery, Suvla Bay.

It was at Gallipoli that LCol. Arthur Lovell Hadow took command of the Newfoundland Regiment. He would remain in charge until December 1917.

The first bravery decorations awarded to the Regiment came as a result of an action that took place on November 4th and 5th, 1915, around a knoll located in "No Man's Land" [area between the two opposing trenches] Suvla Bay. This position was utilized by Turkish snipers to assault whatever moved during the night.

Lieutenant J. J. Donnelly of C Company, a St. John's man who had spent 17 years with the Catholic Cadet Corps before the war, won the prestigious decoration of the Military Cross. Sergeant Walter Greene, a former Newfoundland Constabulary officer and one of the Regiment's "fighting Greene brothers" (Greg and Gus) from Cape Boyle, won the Distinguished Conduct Medal along with Private R.E. Hynes of Indian Island, Fogo. Lance-Corporal Fred Snow of St. John's won the Military Medal.

The knoll where the first bravery decorations were won in Suvla Bay was named Caribou Hill after the brave men of the Newfoundland Regiment who so proudly wore the caribou badges. The four brave men who went down in history for winning the Regiment's first bravery decorations at Suvla were later to give the supreme sacrifice; Captain James J. Donnelly killed at The Battle of Transloy Ridge on October 12, 1916; Lieutenant Walter Greene, killed at The Battle of Cambrai (Marcoing) November 20, 1917 - see poem in appendices; L/Cpl. Fred Snow, and L/Cpl. Richard Hynes both killed at The Battle of Beaumont Hamel on July 1, 1916 .

While the first Newfoundlanders were falling at Suvla, at home in St. John's a big, strapping priest was scratching and fighting to join the Regiment. On October 25, 1915, with the chaplain's appointment eluding him still, Father Tom Nangle squared his Irish jaw, marched down to the recruiting office, and enlisted in the Newfoundland Regiment as a private, an ordinary foot soldier. Adjutant Montgomerie at the recruiting office was obviously taken aback by the desire of the well known clergyman to enlist as a fighting soldier. He immediately contacted his superior, Captain Alan Goodridge, who advised Montgomerie not to swear him in as a private until he heard from the Governor. Davidson's reply to Goodridge was swift and blunt:

> *No ordained Clergyman is to be sworn in as a private in the Newfoundland Regiment without the authority in writing of the official head of his Church. In the case of Father Nangle, the authority must be produced from his Grace the Archbishop of St. John's. I like Father Nangle very much; but it is his first duty to conform to the Discipline of the Church.*

On October 27, 1915, Thomas Nangle wrote to Captain Alan Goodridge regarding his chances of becoming chaplain with the Regiment. He said he had sincere gratitude for all that Goodridge had done in "trying to forward my desire to go the Front as chaplain."

He ended the letter, "I was and still am desirous to serve."

The letter to Goodridge gives insight into Nangle's personality. He was doggedly persistent in his pursuit of a chaplain's appointment even though there were hurdles and road blocks in his way. He was single minded in his desire to go overseas with his friends, school chums and sports teammates. But the road to the Front held yet more roadblocks and pitfalls for the young priest.

The Newfoundland Regiment, along with other allied troops, was evacuated from Suvla Bay on December 20, 1915 and again evacuated from Cape Helles on January 8 and 9, 1916, where it had been acting as part of the rearguard. Our Regiment was the only North American combat unit to fight in the Gallipoli campaign during World War One.

The Gallipoli Campaign proved to be a valuable combat learning experience for the Newfoundland Regiment. As the same time it was an operational experience that was froth with all the negative aspects of warfare; suffering and death, deprivation, pain and suffering from extreme environmental conditions such as frost, sleet, flooding, extreme heat, coupled with severe sickness and disease

On Sunday, January 31, 1916, Father Nangle held Mass at the Cathedral of St. John the Baptist in St. John's for Roman Catholic members of the contingent ready to go to the Front. No one in attendance could have imagined what was to befall the Newfoundland Regiment later that summer.

~ Chapter Five ~
July 1, 1916

The 1st Battalion Newfoundland Regiment was one of four battalions that belonged to the 88th British Infantry Brigade. The 88th was combined with sister units, the 86th and 87th Brigades, to form the 12,000 soldier-strong 29th Infantry Division - a formidable fighting force. The sister battalions of the Newfoundland Regiment as part of the 29th Division were with the 4th Battalion Worcestershire Regiment, 1st Battalion Essex Regiment, and 2nd Battalion Hampshire Regiment.

On Saturday July 1, 1916, the 1st Battalion Newfoundland Regiment stepped out of the safety of the allied trenches and into the pages of history. It was a beautiful summer's day and a clear blue sky looked down from above. This was the start of the Battle of the Somme, a massive British offensive that would last until November 18, 1916. In the coming four and a half months, 250,000 soldiers from nations of the British Empire would be killed.

On July 1, at 8:40 a.m. "the whistles blew and...the Newfoundland Regiment and the 1st Essex were ordered forward to take the first line of enemy trenches." (Cramm, *The First Five Hundred*).

The men of the Newfoundland Regiment began to advance. This was the second wave of the British attack, the first having been repulsed by heavy German fire. As the Newfoundlanders readied themselves for the fray, the sobs and moans of the wounded echoed in their ears.

The Newfoundlanders were crammed into support trenches some three hundred yards or more behind the Allied front line. As they clambered up out of their trenches, the weight of their gear pulled them down as if some unseen hand was trying to hold them in the safety of the dugouts. Military historian Norm Christie described the futile attack of the Newfoundland Regiment:

> *By the time the advance commenced it was 9:15 a.m. and the battlefield was strangely quiet. The only visible movement was the silhouettes of more than 700 Newfoundlanders negotiating around the shell holes and through the barbed wire. The German observers on the overlooking ridges probably could not have believed their eyes. They focused their artillery and machine guns on the small band of approaching men. The fury of the fire must have come like a curtain of death. Soldiers were bowled over by the raining shrapnel explosions; men collapsed as the machine gun bullets tore through them...The Newfoundlanders were being annihilated.*

In less than thirty minutes, 792 soldiers of the Newfoundland Regiment were all but annihilated by German machine gun fire. On that terrible July 1st morning the Regiment suffered 710 casualties.

Sergeant Thomas Carroll is thought to have advanced farther than any Newfoundlander before he was stopped by German steel. General de Lisle of the 29th British Army Division wrote to the Prime Minister of Newfoundland concerning the battle, saying, "It was a magnificent display of trained and disciplined valour, and its assault only failed of success because dead men can advance no further."

The July 1 Battle of Beaumont Hamel was a disaster. Hadow reported the attack had failed at 9:45 a.m. "By 10:20 a.m. the assault had to be given up, and only a defensive line could be held," wrote historian Richard Cramm, while historian Patrick

O'Flaherty noted, "If Gallipoli was Australia's martyrdom, this was Newfoundland's."

On July 2, only 68 soldiers of the Newfoundland Regiment were present for roll call.

The casualty list, as researched by regimental historian David Parsons, was staggering: 438 wounded, of whom 29 later died; 133 killed in action; 139 missing and presumed dead. Missing could mean captured, shot and the body unrecovered from the battlefield, or it could mean blown to pieces by artillery fire. So fierce was the fighting of the First World War that a great many soldiers were simply missing in action and presumed dead.

Ninety per cent of the Newfoundland Regiment were casualties after the advance on July 1, according to historian Norm Christie. In fact, during the entire war, the Newfoundland Regiment suffered the highest casualty rate (27 percent) of all British Forces serving on the Western Front. Along the entire Front on July 1, the British Army suffered 57,540 casualties, including 19,200 estimated killed. It was the worst day in British army history.

News of the great tragedy at Beaumont Hamel slowly began to make its way to Newfoundland, like an evening tide creeping ashore. But it wasn't until July 13th that a full list of the casualties became known to people in Newfoundland.

Among those gathered outside the post office on Water Street in St. John's that day was Dutch landscape architect Rudolph Cochius, who had lived and worked in the city for years while creating Bowring Park for Sir Edgar Bowring. He described the crowds waiting to learn the names of those killed in action on July 1st:

I saw that tense and silent crowd patiently, yet impatiently, waiting in front of the Post Office and the bulletins elsewhere on Water Street, in anxious apprehension, scanning each successive telegram that appeared - some to receive the news they feared most, some to await with stimulated hope some later bulletin.

As news of the tragedy slowly reached Newfoundland one can only imagine that Father Tom Nangle's desire to go the Front to be with his friends and fellow countrymen intensified.

On July 2, 1916, the battlefield fell quiet, as the Germans allowed an informal truce to permit the British to remove the wounded and hurriedly bury their dead. "The surviving Newfoundlanders had to bury many of their friends," wrote Cramm. For the next three months, the Newfoundlanders would be in rest camps and the Regiment brought up to strength.

On July 15, 1916 *The Daily News* issued a short statement that a chaplain had been appointed to the Roman Roman Catholic section of the Newfoundland Regiment.

Archbishop Roche of St. John's quickly fired off a letter to Governor Davidson indicating that *The Daily News* story was incorrect and that no chaplain had been appointed. Roche said Father Nangle was anxious to take work as a military chaplain and as there was no opening in that direction here, he was permitting him to leave the diocese.

One wonders, what part, if any, Nangle may have played in *The Daily News* story. Roche's letter gave the impression that Nangle would be leaving St. John's, but certainly not as chaplain to the Newfoundland Regiment.

A day later, on July 16, 1916, Archbishop Roche penned another letter to Governor Davidson:

> *I have to acknowledge your communication of yesterday's date and also the telegram from the Secretary of State announcing that Father Nangle had been accepted by the War Office as Chaplain. I have no objection to his being attached to the Regiment for the purpose of passage nor his wearing the prescribed uniform of a military chaplain whilst he is so attached. It is due to Your Excellency's great kindness that the matter has ended so satisfactorily and I trust Father Nangle's career as Chaplain with the army will justify the kindly interest you have taken in his case.*

On July 18, 1916 the Archbishop drafted a letter permitting Father Nangle to leave the diocese and carry on his journey to the Front. The letter said the Newfoundland government had not attached any chaplains to the Regiment. Roche went on to say he hoped it "may be possible for him (Nangle) to be with the Roman Catholic soldiers of the Newfoundland Regiment."

On that same day, the Archbishop penned another letter for Nangle, this one a letter of introduction:

> *Rev. Thomas Nangle was ordained for this Archdiocese of St. John's in June 1913. Since that time he laboured in various Missions in the Diocese and has performed all his sacerdotal duties with satisfaction. He is a total abstainer and his priestly character is in every way above reproach.*

The Archbishop pointed out that Nangle had volunteered his services for the British Army. He asked all "Ordinaries of all Dioceses in which he may happen to be...to accord him the privilege of offering up the holy sacrifice of Mass."

The appointment of Nangle as chaplain less than three weeks after the bloody "July Drive" was likely no mere coincidence. The staggering losses suffered by the Newfoundlanders at Beaumont Hamel drove home the need for chaplains to attend to the spiritual needs of the crippled, wounded and dying, as well as the survivors.

Reverend Arthur C. Clayton enlisted in March 1916 and ministered to the needs of the Church of England in the Regiment. Thomas Nangle would serve alongside Padre Clayton and minister to the Roman Catholics. Nangle would stay for the duration of the war, Clayton served a little over one year up until May 1917. In June 1917, Padre Clayton was replaced by Reverend G. H. Maidment.

Nangle's appointment as Temporary Chaplain (4th class) was effective August 15, 1916. However, his excitement at being appointed a chaplain was tempered by the winds of fate. His beloved mother died on November 1916.

According to an obituary in *The Daily News* of November 27, 1916, the then Mrs. Murphy passed away at her residence on Topsail Road after a lengthy illness. She was described as,

> *A woman of strong character, gentle and loving and with a charitable nature that made her an ideal mother, wife and friend. She was beloved by the large community that knew her, who will learn with sorrow of her death. Her passing brings a more profound sadness because of the absence of her only child, Father Nangle now somewhere in France ministering to the wants of the brave soldiers defending the Empire; whose one wish would be to be at the deathbed of his saintly mother. To Chaplain Nangle, a stream of sympathy will follow from the homeland to far off France, from thousands of friends together with the belief that his burden will be lightened by Him who called him to priesthood and to blood stained fields to minister to the dying far from home and friends, and whose mothers*

would have liked to close their chilled hands or kiss their pallid cheeks when the supreme sacrifice had been made. To Father Nangle, Mr. Murphy and other members of the family, the News joins in the general and sincere sympathy expressed.

Priests have been going into battle for centuries. Chaplains have been in existence since at least 1066 when William, Duke of Normandy, took along some priests on his invasion of Britain, according to information posted on the website of the Royal Army Chaplains Department. The British established its Army Chaplain's Department in 1796. The qualities required of a chaplain were: "Zeal in his profession and good sense, gentle manners; a distinctive and impressive manner of reading Divine Service; a firm constitution of body as well as of mind." Tom Nangle undoubtedly had the required zeal as he doggedly pursued a chaplain's appointment. And years of school athletics had hardened his muscles and body.

Hagerty's research on chaplains notes that all new chaplains were "introduced to military organization, command structures and customs." This would have been easy fare for Nangle to digest since he had been part of the Roman Catholic Cadet Corps.

Hagerty says too that nothing was "laid down in Army regulations about the duty of a chaplain except that he was generally speaking to seek the spiritual and moral welfare of the men of his denomination...the methods adopted by chaplains were left to individual initiative..."

Father Nangle was initially attached to the 101st Field Ambulance unit of the 88th Brigade, British Expeditionary Force. He soon found himself at the Front and in short order had a taste of the horror of trench warfare.

In one of his first telegrams home, he sketched the sudden, unexpected loss of life in the trenches to the family of

Lieutenant Stephen Norris.

TO: Jas. Norris, c/o Jackman, Water Street, St. John's

Steve killed eleven A.M. October 11 by big shell. Whole trench fell in body not found. Am on the ground myself doing everything possible to locate body. All were at Confession day before. Donnelly shot on German Parapet; O'Brien wounded - stomach lived for week. Am longside Our Boys. Heartfelt sympathy to self, Mother Nell and Family.

Signed Tom Nangle

His letter gives insight to the awful losses that befell Newfoundlanders on the Western Front of Europe. It also gives an idea of how 91 men could be missing after Beaumont Hamel.

The letter also contains Nangle's fond reference to "Our Boys." Throughout his tenure on the Western Front, he always referred to the Newfoundland Regiment as "Our Boys" or simply "Ours." He spoke of all Newfoundland soldiers in this manner, without distinguishing between Roman Catholics and other denominations.

"It was in the willingness of most Roman Catholic padres to share the privations and dangers of trench, warship and battle that earned them...a respect not easily won," says Hagerty. This was doubtless true of Father Tom Nangle who was in the trenches with the men, and who would eventually get "trench foot" and be wounded in the shoulder.

On October 12, 1916, men of the 1st Battalion Newfoundland Regiment, and 1st Battalion Essex Regiment attacked the German trenches near Gueudecourt, France. The attack on Gueudecourt, says Christie, was similar to earlier advances in the Battle of the Somme in that it "gained little ground, but had cost the attackers thousands of men."

Cramm notes, however, that, "Captain March displayed great ability and calm resourcefulness in the face of very great danger. He took a leading part in the first attack and is credited with having bayoneted three Germans."

For his actions March was awarded the Military Cross and French Croix de Guerre. In addition to March's decorations at Gueudecourt, other members of the Regiment won a total of three Distinguished Conduct medals, five Military Medals and one Bar to the Military Cross.

Father Tom Nangle joined the Newfoundland Regiment on the last of October in Ville-sur-Ancre, known to the Newfoundlanders as "Ville."

> *It was at Ville that Captain Tom Nangle came to the Regiment as Roman Catholic Chaplain. A man of boundless enthusiasm, he became popular with all the troops, regardless of denomination, and made an outstanding contribution to the morale of the Battalion. (Nicholson, The Fighting Newfoundlander)*

Private Anthony James Stacey, Regimental #466, was at Ville when Nangle arrived. In his memoirs, he recalled it was late and acting Padre Stenlake, who was in charge of buying all refreshments, including alcoholic beverages, was in bed.

> *There he (Stenlake) was with a case of whiskey at his head for safety and a bag of prayer books at his feet. Padre Nangle remarked smiling, "I don't know what religion is coming to, a clergyman has a case of whiskey under his head and a bag of prayer books at his feet." (Memoirs of a Blue Puttee).*

(Stenlake had been evacuated from Suvla due to illness on November 26, 1915. He was invalided to England on January 3, 1916.)

Padre Nangle was seen as a congenial type by all the men whom he served. Captain Leo Murphy commented on his amiable nature in *The Veteran* magazine in 1921.

> ....It's dark in the dugout-the candle burns low! Comes a heavy step and a cheerful voice! A stalwart form darkens the entrance and makes itself known...It is 'Padre Nangle'; beloved of the Regiment and always welcome for his genial personality and pleasant company. "A Hun plane is overhead," he says, and we are instantly on our feet and out into the trench, warning the men against unnecessary movement...

The German plane that was overhead crashed. Nangle, Herb Rendell and John Edens ran to the crash site and saw that the two occupants of the plane had died on impact. The propellor blade was found some ten feet away. Nangle later presented the propellor to the Benevolent Irish Society in St. John's, after it had been fitted out with a clock and a weather glass.

In early November 1916, Nangle wrote to Archbishop Roche informing him he had been appointed chaplain of the Newfoundland Regiment. At long last he had achieved his goal!

In Ville, eighteen second lieutenants were added to the Regiment, giving an idea of the staggering losses being suffered among all ranks. In short order, Father Nangle began to pray over the dying and bury the dead from his native soil. He would have known many of these men personally from school and sports competitions in St. John's, and traveling with them on the lengthy voyage from St. John's to Europe.

Soon, he would also be engaged in the gruesome work of locating the fallen and helping identify and bury them. At times, he gave the Last Rites to body parts- all that remained of men hit directly by artillery fire or cut to pieces by machine gun bursts. After the war, these scattered remains were exhumed from their hurried battlefield graves and re-interred in proper military cemeteries.

In a three page letter to Governor Davidson, dated December 19, 1916, Padre Nangle wrote about his work locating the remains of the Newfoundland war dead scattered over the length of the Beaumont Hamel battlefield:

> Your Excellency,
> Having received over two hundred letters of enquiry from relatives and friends of our gallant lads who died on the 1st of July, it is impossible for me to answer all, so I thought it better to advise you of the graves I found....
>
> The first place I came to was Auchonvillers, and here I found a little graveyard close to the ruined Church. It looked a quiet little place, surrounded by trees and adorned with wild flowers, but I soon changed my opinion for before I left the spot I had to hop into an unoccupied grave where I listened to the music of a maxim[machine-gun] as its bullets went zip zip through the trees. Many of the crosses are riddled particularly that over the grave of Sergt. Gus Manning. At the head of this little cemetery...rest seven of ours: 2/lieut. Grant and Pte. E.C. Whitten (in one grave); Sergt. A.J. Manning; Pte. Knight, Pte. Fray and Pte. Perrin (in one grave) and Pte. P. Eagan.
>
> Turning south east I tramped on through Tipperary Avenue [communication trench]...and I found...
>
> Knightsbridge Military Cemetery....were it not for the bark of our guns, almost hidden in their pits, one would think he was on "Brigus Barrens" for even in this God foresaken place one finds numerous coveys of the timid partridge.
>
> The cemetery is on a gentle slope facing east to Beaumont Hamel, and here rest 28 sons of Newfoundland....All those

men were buried either by Rev. Mr. C.H. Mosse or Canon Reid both C. Of E. Chaplains, the former of whom is still with the 88th Brigade...Not far from Knightsbridge there is a French Military Cemetery and there I found the grave of 1587 Pte.J. Curnew who was sniped 24 April....I wish some of our young men at home could have stood by my side...and gaze on these graves...but oh they were eloquent - the call, the sacrifice, the hard months of training, the separation from home and loved ones, the privations of the campaign, and then the grand climax - the sacrifice of their noble lives in order that we at home may live in peace. Those men were heroes. Ours was a Regiment of heroes...I am writing this letter Your Excellency to advise you of the graves where our heroes lie buried. You may have an opportunity of informing their parents and thereby lessen the pangs of grief by the knowledge that their boys had Christian burial and that they or friends, in happier days, may visit the historic spot in this far off land.

> *I remain,*
> *Yours respectfully,*
> *T. Nangle*
> *1st Batt. Nfld. Regiment*

The Newfoundland Regiment remained in the Gueudecourt area until December. The remaining days of 1916, and almost all of the first month of 1917 were spent in rest camps. At Christmas, says Nicholson, "Padre Nangle undertook the management of a joint officer's dinner in the Battalion Headquarter's mess."

Nangle played an important role in the celebration of Christmas that year. He undoubtedly held Mass for the Roman Catholic men, and his warm personality and deep faith were an inspiration for war-weary soldiers of all denominations.

~ Chapter Six ~

THE WAR CONTINUES

During the month of January 1917, "1st Battalion, the Newfoundland Regiment, spent much of the time training and assimilating new recruits," says historian Norm Christie.

In February 1917, Nicholson notes there was some fun as Padre Nangle helped organize and played in a hockey game on a frozen village duck pond, an example of his efforts at boosting morale and trying to take the men's minds off the war for a brief time.

In a March 9, 1917, letter to Major Timewell, Chief Paymaster and Officer-in-Charge-of-Records for the Regiment, Nangle said, "I shall be only too happy to answer any letter of enquiry concerning any of our boys or do anything to help..."

Disease, Dirt and Filth

In another letter to Timewell, dated March 21, 1917, Nangle noted that a member of the Regiment named Oliphant was in hospital with rheumatism. While death could fly suddenly and unexpectedly from the sniper's bullet, or a high-explosive artillery shell, day in and day out sickness and disease, filth and squalor were the trench soldier's constant companion. Rheumatism, pneumonia, lice, rats, trench foot, dysentery and enteritis were common and sapped the strength and morale of men struggling to survive day to day.

In the trenches at Gallipoli, historian Richard Cramm says "dysentery and enteric played havoc with the entire forces...many of our men were invalided to hospitals...few escaped the disease entirely, many died from its effects."

More about the terrible conditions in the trenches was reported by Private Francis Lind, "two of our fellows died of dysentery, Lance Corporal Watts... and Pte. Walter Murphy," he wrote in an October 13, 1915 letter to *The Daily News*.

In his book "Trenching at Gallipoli" Corporal John Gallishaw wrote about his experiences at Suvla Bay, saying "the trenches where we slept harbored not only rats but vermin and all manner of things foul."

Lind too talked about the constant problem of rats in the trenches. In a June 29, 1916, letter to *The Daily News* he said rats were even crawling over sleeping men.

Rats infested the trenches in millions, gorging themselves on human remains, disfiguring them in the process, according to website www.firstworldwar.com. Lice infested the filthy clothes of weary warriors and were hard to get rid of even after the occasional wash and delousing. Many men kept their heads shaved to avoid "nits."

Back to the Front

On May 31, 1917, Governor Davidson, Colonel of the Regiment, wrote to Father Nangle at the Front:

> *My Dear Father Nangle,*
> *I have not heard from you as often as I should like but what*
> *I have heard of you proves once again how wise a thing it was*
> *to further your desire to be in the battle.*
> *General Cayley in a personal letter praises you much...I*

wish you the best of luck and the opportunity to continue your good work.

> *From the bottom of my heart I am*
> *Yours sincerely,*
> *Davidson*

Davidson was probably worried about Nangle because in mid-April that year the Regiment had attacked the German defenses near Monchy-le-Preux. The action cost the Newfoundlanders 166 killed, 141 wounded and 150 taken prisoner.

It was in this action that LCol. Forbes-Robertson and eight soldiers of the Newfoundland Regiment and one of the Essex Regiment held the village of Monchy against a German counter-attack. The men credited with saving Monchy were: LCol. James Forbes-Roberston; Lieutenant Kevin Keegan; Corporal Albert Rose; Corporal John Hillier; Sergeant Charles Parsons; Sergeant Ross Waterfield; Private Japheth Hounsell; Sergeant Walter Pitcher; Private Fred Curran; and Private V.M. Parsons of the Essex Regiment.

The men known as "The Ten Heroes of Monchy" are referred to in official British history as "all that stood between the Germans and Monchy, one of the most vital positions in the whole battlefield."

Forbes-Robertson was commanding officer of the Newfoundland Regiment in 1917 and went on to win a Victoria Cross in France in April of 1918 while serving with the Border Regiment.

On June 13, 1917, Davidson wrote to Nangle again, saying, "I have not heard from you for a long time but I have heard a good deal of you and it has all been to your honour. Captain Clayton [the Church of England Padre] praises you highly..."

The Newfoundlanders were launched into another bloody offensive on July 31, 1917. This was known as the Third Battle of Ypres, or the Passchendale Campaign.

The Newfoundlanders began advancing near the Steenbeek River and the Regiment was forced to cross an incredibly difficult piece of ground which was hardly more than a floating swamp. During the action, many members of the Regiment distinguished themselves, including Cpl. H. Raynes who was awarded the Distinguished Conduct Medal and the French Croix de Guerre. The losses to the Regiment included nine killed, 93 wounded and one missing.

On September 11, 1917, His Eminence Cardinal Logue wrote The Irish Press about the chaplains' work along the Front and indicated there was a lack of Roman Catholic chaplains. He said in France the War Office acknowledged it was short 93 Roman Catholic chaplains. Many chaplains were retiring from exhaustion and there were woefully few priests volunteering for war service.

By the end of the summer of 1917, Nangle had been with the Regiment for almost one year. On September 21, 1917, he embarked from Liverpool aboard the Scotian for his first leave away from the Front.

In a letter written aboard ship, he told a comrade about a Christmas card he was having designed for the Regiment. This correspondence is an example of Nangle's devotion to the men in the trenches and the families at home. Although he was on leave, he was planning for another lonely Christmas at the Front where soldiers and their loved ones were separated by the Atlantic Ocean. He realized that something as simple as a Christmas card could help alleviate the fears and worries of family at home.

Having them would also free soldiers from the almost impossible burden of finding a Christmas card to send home. Of course, it would be a great morale booster for the men to have distinctive Regimental Christmas cards.

Nangle wanted the caribou head to appear on the card "the exact size and color of the cap badge." He also wanted to get Colonel Hadow's approval of the Christmas card design and cost. He told his colleague in London that he hoped Hadow would sign off on the design and cost to have 5,000 cards printed and delivered to France before November 25th.

A sad footnote to the Christmas card project is that while the cards were printed, they were unfortunately blown to pieces when a French railway station was bombed. In "Memoirs of a Blue Puttee," A.J. Stacey describes how he had charge of a large backlog of parcel mail, including the Christmas cards for the troops. However, because the railway tracks were blown at a station along the way, all mail had to be carried by hand almost half a mile to another train. Because there wasn't enough time much of the mail was left behind, including the Christmas cards.

> *As the train was pulling away Major Bernard came on the scene and said, "Stacey, all the mail aboard?" What could I say? He knew by time and distance it was impossible to have moved it all and by the look on his face was joking, so I answered with a smile, "It's all aboard, sir."...I was told that the Christmas cards were seen blowing around after the railway was bombed. They were printed especially for the Regiment with a caribou head embossed in gold. They were to be given to the boys to send home Christmas greetings.*

On October 1, 1917, Major Timewell, Chief Paymaster and Officer-in-Charge of Records, wrote the Minister of the Militia in St. John's enquiring whether the cost of Father Nangle's transport to St. John's was to be recovered from him or charged to Newfoundland public funds. The purpose of his visit to St. John's was to have a furlough from the rigors of the combat zone.

On October 9, 1917, the 29th Division took part in the Battle of Poelcapelle. The British attack was along a 10 kilometer front with a total of 13 Divisions involved.

The Newfoundlanders, as part of the 29th Division, and their comrades fought forward through knee-deep mud and achieved gains of almost two kilometers. Historian Norm Christie says the action cost another 127 Newfoundlanders wounded or killed in action. Among the dead was Lieutenant Stanley Goodyear, who had previously won a Military Cross for gallantry in action. Goodyear's two brothers, Oswald and Hedley, were also killed in separate actions.

The Home Front

Padre Nangle's good reputation with soldiers of all denominations at the Front made him an obvious choice to do some recruiting while he was home in St. John's on furlough.

On October 12, 1917, the Minister of the Militia, John R. Bennett, wrote to Archbishop Roche concerning Nangle's potential involvement in recruiting soldiers for the war effort:

Your Grace,
> *Those charged with the care, responsibility and upkeep of the Newfoundland Regiment are desirous of using every possible means available to secure sufficient recruits to maintain our Regiment as a separate unit.*
> *Recruiting parties are being formed to visit all parts of the colony. In the formation of those parties it is most essential that the services of Officers and men, who have been at the Front, should be utilized....Standing out prominently*

amongst those is Rev. Capt. Nangle, at present home on leave. May I...approach Your Grace with a view to obtaining your sanction for Father Nangle to assist us in this work. I understand from him that he is quite prepared to help us if Your Grace will sanction it.

> *Your Grace's*
> *Humble Servant*
> *Hon. J. Bennett*
> *Minister of Militia*

Archbishop Roche's reply was just three days in coming. In a letter dated October 15, 1917, he dismissed Bennett's plea to have Father Nangle undertake recruiting work:

My Dear Mr. Bennett,
> *I have to acknowledge receipt of your letter of October 12th with reference to obtaining the assistance of Father Nangle in the approaching recruiting campaign....I regret that I cannot see my way clear to acquiesce in the suggestion contained in your letter. I do not think...the work of recruiting would be in keeping with a Clergyman's position...In the second place, Father Nangle's services as a Chaplain with the troops are urgently needed at this present time. The demand for more Chaplains is becoming stronger and more insistent all the time...Father Nangle's first and foremost duty as a Roman Catholic Chaplain is with our soldiers at the Front....*

> *I remain*
> *Faithfully yours,*
> *E. P. Roche*

So it seemed that Father Tom Nangle was not going to be doing any recruiting work while on leave. But like the old saying, "things are not always what they seem."

Torpeod'd - Destroyed Cape Helles, Gallipoli

"The Hill of Fame" Nangle in dugout fortified area, Caribou Hill, Suvla, Gallipoli.

Colonel A.L. Hadow, LCol. Forbes - Robertson.

Men who saved Monchy.

"Blue Puttees Sergeants.

Padre The Rev. G.H. Maidment

Road scene after clean-up on The Western Front.

Typical mud scene on The Western Front.

One of the most dangerous places during WWI, Hellfire Corner.

Surviving Officers Arras 1917, Nangle 2nd from the left standing.

LCol. Nangle with Mayor of Beaumont Hamel and others viewing crater.

Ecquires, British Expeditionary Force General Headquarters

La Poupee - Scene of many happy moments...
Poperinghe-Hotel & Restaurant, Belgium.

Battalion returning from Arras.

Ingoyghen - Furthest advance of Regiment in Belgium.

Nangle overseeing graves exhumation party (France)

H.M. King George V accompanied by Sir Edgar Bowring at Newfoundland graveside in Etaples British Cemetery 1922

Haig visit party July, 1924 at Bannerman Park uniform members (L to R) Haig, Nangle, Bennett, Whitty in background.

Caribou Memorial under construction in Europe.

SOLDIER - PRIEST IN THE KILLING FIELDS OF EUROPE, WW I:

Early graves.

Early grave site of Pte. Zechariah Blake.

Newfoundland temorary grave

"RIP" Pic of early grave site of Pte. Max Thompson.

Pte. Morris' grave

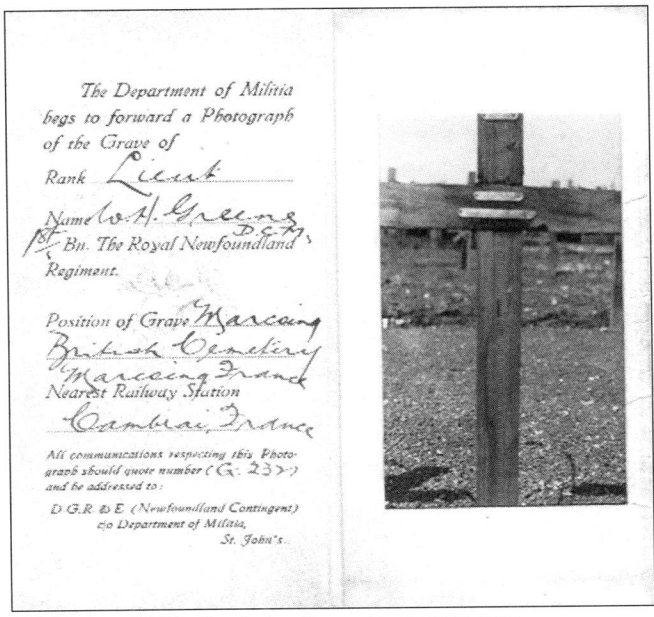

Notification for families and temporary grave.

Covered with shellcasings, Capt. James Donnelly's grave, killed Oct. 12, 1916 near Gueudecourt.

Early grave site of Pte. R. Little.

Sir Alexander Haig

Where the Battalion crossed at Cambrai.

Notice board from Council of Ypres concerning sacred ground where 250 British died.

Central monument Wandsworth Hospital Cemetery, England.

Bridge where 30 of 'Ours' fell, Cambrai 1917.

Reflecting the optimistic Tommy - bombed out building, France.

Newfoundland Prime Minister, Sir Richard Squires, his wife and daughter, the driver and LCol Nangle - France.

Nangle fund raiser for National War Memorial.

Excavating a Newfoundland soldier's grave - France.

SOLDIER - PRIEST IN THE KILLING FIELDS OF EUROPE, WW I:

The fate of Big Bertha the gun that shelled Paris, Nangle sitting - Coaker far right.

Barrel of "Big Bertha" gun.

Capt. Whitty's funeral in St. John's, 1924. (Whitty was Secretary of Great War Veteran's Assoc., Newfoundland)

Captain Gerald J. Whitty, O.B.E., M.C. close friend of Nangle

Field Marshal Haig, ADC Nangle at St. George's Field, St. John's - Haig visit 1924

Haig and Nangle talking to veterans at waterfront, St. John's - Haig visit 1924

Prime Minister Richard Squires accepting Fencibles Colours in Trust, old Newfoundland Museum.

Early war graves cemetery.

~ Chapter Seven ~

RECRUITING

With his mind and spirit still with his boys at the Front, Nangle gave a speech to a standing room only crowd in the Casino Theatre in St. John's, reportedly on the night before he was to set sail for Europe. Going against the orders of Archbishop Roche he rolled up his sleeves and got busy recruiting.

He tried to give some idea of what the fighting was like at the Front. He also appealed for men to sign up and join the fray. The fact that he went ahead and spoke publicly about the war effort and went against the written orders of the Archbishop suggests he had a strong commitment to and belief in the justness of the war effort. It also hints at his strong personality and willingness to disobey orders to do what he felt was right. Archbishop Roche, for reasons unknown, did not attend Father Nangle's lecture.

A writer who heard the speech said afterwards, "If Captain Nangle could be heard in the halls and schools throughout our Island, there would be few of military age and ability who would fail to respond to the Empire's call."

Nangle spoke of the bombardment of Gueudecourt and how the Newfoundlanders' success was the only real British success in that action:

> *The boys before going over the trenches took off their puttees and stuck their long pants down into Newfoundland socks,*

> *leaving their puttees in the trenches. They went over the embankment with a yell. Some of them had on skin boots...Edens had a narrow escape. A German came upon him within five yards and fired at him point blank. The bullet went between his arm and body, punching two holes in his tunic, his sweater and his shirt but did not touch the arm itself. Before the German could draw his trigger again, Edens had dealt with him and there was one German less to fight...*

Nangle used wit, humor and Newfoundland references to explain the war and the need for volunteers:

> *Part of his popularity arose from his skill incorporating local references in his stories. He described the old style gas helmet as a regular mummer's outfit, which would frighten everyone at the Christmas season and quoted this exchange between an officer and a private: "What are you?" asked the officer...a bombardier or a grenadier?" "Neither," came the unexpected reply, "I'm a bayman." He made a passionate plea for recruits lamenting the fact Blue Puttees were unable to come home for want of volunteers.* (Encyclopedia of Newfoundland and Labrador)

"Father Nangle's influence in encouraging recruiting can never be estimated and should never be undervalued. He was one of those who saw the need and spoke out, and what he said bore fruit," reported the March 1919 issue of *The Newfoundland Magazine*.

Back to the Front

The day after delivering his address at the Casino Theatre, Nangle boarded ship and began the journey back to the boys in the trenches.

On November 20, 1917, the Newfoundland Regiment and their comrades in the 29th Division took part in a history making action - the Battle of Cambrai. Under command of

General Sir Julian Byng, the British attacked the German lines using a combination of infantry and a massive array of tanks. This was the first time that tanks were used so prominently in battle.

Padre Nangle's main concern was with those who had fallen in the recent fighting, according to Nicholson. With a party of men, Nangle scoured the area surrounding the lock and the road along the [St.Quentin] Canal. The bodies of dead Newfoundlanders were collected and carried back to the edge of Marcoing Copse, where they were interred in a temporary cemetery. One of the fallen soldiers whom Nagle buried was Lieutenant Walter Greene of Cape Broyle, a brave young officer who had won the Regiment's first bravery award, the Distinguished Conduct Medal, at Gallipoli in 1915, and who was seriously wounded just prior to the Battle of the Somme in June of 1916.

Lieutenant John Edens was killed alongside Greene. Edens had written a letter to his parents on November 19, the day before his death, saying he had gone to confession and would "go over the top with the consolation of religion."

During this same period [November 23rd], Padre Nangle oversaw the burial of Corporal John Shiwak, an Inuit hunter and trapper from Rigolet, Labrador. Shiwak and six others from the Regiment were killed by an exploding shell during an attack on the village of Masnieres on November 21st, 1917. Cpl. Shiwak impressed all as an excellent scout and marksman. One officer referred to him as the best sniper in the British Army. Shiwak was a very shy and quiet man. Friends he made in France included Newfoundlander Howard L. Morry, whose unpublished memoirs describe "Johnny Shirvack" as "a sniper and a good one." Said Morry: "He was shy and lonely but I got to be quite friendly with him by talking about seal hunting, etc. We'd talk for hours and often he'd say, 'when will it ever be over?' He said sniping was like swatching seals." [Dictionary of

Canadian Biography] Shiwak was buried in the village of Masnieres, but after the war his grave was unable to be found. This is an example of one of the many frustrations referred to by Padre Nangle when he was trying to find and identify remains after the war.

On the evening of November 29, 1917, the Newfoundland Regiment received orders to carry out a relief in front of Masinieres. At dawn the next morning the Germans began heavily shelling the town. The "German great counter-attack burst forth in all its fury," says Cramm. Historian Norm Christie described this action as the Newfoundland Regiment's "most critical fight of the war." The Regiment held their positions and drove the enemy back to Marcoing, but the fighting was terrific.

From December 1st to December 3rd, 1917, the Germans shelled the Newfoundland positions. On December 3, the Newfoundlanders were withdrawn, surrendering the territory to the Germans. Between November 30th and December 3rd, 57 Newfoundlanders were killed, and Christie says the graves of 54 were never found or identified.

During the entire Battle of Cambrai, from November 20th when the battle started, until the Newfoundlanders were withdrawn on December 3rd, the Regiment suffered 462 casualties, including, says Christie, more than one hundred killed.

Padre Nangle was with the Regiment during this action which failed to capture Cambrai. He helped gather bodies and gave them battlefield burials.

Christie says when "the Battle of Cambrai officially ended on [December 7th]...it had cost the British 38,000 killed and wounded and 6,000 prisoners."

Cramm describes the heroics of the Newfoundland Regiment in this action as "magnificent" and as something the "survivors of the Battalion could look back over...with entire satisfaction."

The bravery of the Newfoundland Regiment during the Battle of Cambrai did not go unnoticed. During the action at Masnieres, no fewer than 27 members of the Newfoundland Regiment were decorated for bravery in action. For holding the British line at Masnieres, King George V of England honoured the Newfoundland Regiment by granting it the prefix Royal:

> *The King has been pleased to grant the title of Royal to the Newfoundland Regiment. This distinction comes as a fitting tribute to the loyal and ancient Colony, whose sons have fought so well and in so many battles. It is the first instance of such a title being conferred in the present war.*

Newfoundland was a non-military country in 1914 and raised her Regiment, her Royal Naval Reserve and her Forestry Corps entirely by voluntary enlistment. It speaks well for the fighting qualities of the Newfoundlanders that the Regiment was attached to one of the most famous divisions in the British Army - "the Immortal 29th." The Newfoundlanders took part in the fighting in Gallipoli, the Somme, Arras, Ypres, and Cambrai.

In the entire First World War, the Newfoundland Regiment was the only unit to be honoured with the granting of the title "Royal."

Around the same time that the Newfoundland Regiment became the Royal Newfoundland Regiment, incoming Governor Sir Charles Harris announced that "Newfoundland had been elevated to the rank of 'a first class Colony or Dominion' equal in status to Canada, Australia, New Zealand

and South Africa," says historian Patrick O'Flaherty, who maintains that Newfoundland was so honored "principally because of the bravery of the Regiment."

Christmas 1917

On December 4, 1917, Padre Nangle sent the following telegram to Chief Paymaster Major Timewell concerning the Furness-Withy shipping line which operated between Liverpool, Boston and St. John's:

> *Just a line as we are on the move. Would you kindly phone Furness-Withy people to know if they have seen anything of the men's Christmas gifts....I expect will be out for Christmas.*

"The Regiment is on its way to rest and is just about 300 strong all told," Nangle wrote a friend on December 5, 1917.

The heavy fighting of November and December had taken its toll on the Regiment. Sadly, Father Nangle had been very busy burying the dead, anointing the dying, consoling the wounded and writing to families of the fallen.

The Newfoundlanders enjoyed Christmas dinner at the village of Fressen that year. Father Nangle likely said Mass and held Confessions. Christmas Day, says Cramm, was "a much enjoyed day, the other side of a soldier's life."

~ Chapter Eight ~

WOUNDED

The Newfoundland Regiment was rebuilt during the winter months, its numbers increased by a draft of 172 reinforcements. Near the third week of March 1918, the German Army launched a huge offensive.

In the mid-April Battle of Bailleul, the Newfoundland Regiment counter-attacked German positions near Steenwerck. According to Christie, the Newfoundlanders held their gains for two days before being ordered to make a fighting retreat.

In this two day action, Cramm reports there were 50 Newfoundlanders killed, 133 wounded and 16 who went missing in action. Padre Nangle was with the Regiment, tending to the needs of wounded, dead and dying.

As a result of the severe losses in April, the Newfoundlanders were withdrawn from the line and pulled from the ranks of the 29th Division. "I wish to place on record my very great regret at their withdrawal from a division in which they have served so long and brilliantly," said Major-General D. Cayley, Commander of the 29th.

On April 24, 1918, Padre Nangle was wounded in action. He was hit in the shoulder and apparently sent to London to recuperate. Having been so close to the Front for so long, it is amazing he wasn't killed. During the war, according to Hagerty, a total of 172 chaplains of all denominations gave their lives, including 36 Roman Catholic chaplains.

Nangle was not a man to stay in the rear. He was with his boys in the trenches with the shrapnel and bullets flying. Later in life, although he complained of a bad shoulder, Hugh Nangle said his father never told his children that he had been wounded in action.

Nangle also developed "trench foot," a common fungal ailment among the soldiers. In the trenches one's feet were almost always wet and dirty. The unhygienic conditions were fertile ground for disease.

Final Battles

The Newfoundland Regiment was to be a part of the final Allied advance in late 1918. In September of that year, the Regiment was re-mobilized for fighting as part of the 9th Scottish Division, commanded by General Hugh Tudor. General Tudor later settled in St. John's, where he died in 1965.

On September 28, 1918, at 5:30 a.m. the 9th Division cut into enemy lines. By now, says Christie, most of the Newfoundland Regiment consisted of inexperienced troops. The Newfoundlanders followed the main advance and suffered only slight casualties. The next day, the Newfoundlanders advanced over the Keiberg Ridge and met heavy German resistance. Men began to fall to withering machine-gun fire. But over two days, the Newfoundland Regiment advanced 14 kilometers. "The advance during these two days again brought out the fighting qualities with which the Royal Newfoundland Regiment was endowed," says Cramm.

In October, the Newfoundlanders captured Ledeghem (Ledegem). According to Christie, in the early morning on October 14, 1918, the Newfoundland Regiment began to advance from its positions in Ledeghem. By the end of the day the Regiment advanced 5 kilometers at a cost of 26 men wounded or killed.

That day is special in the history of the Regiment because Private Thomas "Tommy" Ricketts, a 17-year-old from Middle Arm, White Bay, won the Victoria Cross for his brave actions to re-supply a machine-gun with ammunition. Ricketts was the only winner of the Victoria Cross from the Regiment during the entire war. He was also one of only two Newfoundlanders to win the prestigious honour. The other Victoria Cross winner was John Bernard Croke of Little Bay, who was fighting with the Canadian Army. Father Nangle described Rickett's brave action:

> *Private T. Ricketts went forward with his section commander, and a Lewis Gun, with a view to outflanking the (German) battery; but when they were still 300 yards away from the enemy they ran short of ammunition, and the Germans, hoping to save their guns, brought up the teams. Thereupon Private Ricketts darted back under a fierce fire from machine-guns with the battery, procured more ammunition, and returned at the double to the Lewis Gun, which he fired with such accuracy that the Germans with their gun teams were compelled to take refuge in a farm. The rest of the platoon was now able to press on without casualties, and 4 field guns and 8 prisoners were taken. Subsequently a fifth field-gun was intercepted by our fire and captured.*

Members of the Regiment involved in the same action were awarded two Military Crosses, a Bar to the Military Cross, six Distinguished Conduct Medals, nine Military Medals and one Bar to the Military Medal, says Cramm. The Newfoundlanders were in the thick of the action and proved themselves excellent soldiers at Ledgehem.

Around the time that Private Ricketts won his Victoria Cross, Father Nangle wrote to Major Timewell that he was back with the boys again and still going strong. He had totally recovered from his wound and was glad to be once again back at the Front.

A Married Man?

During the period when Nangle was rejoining the Regiment, he was being investigated by the military. A rumor had begun to circulate that Father Nangle had become a "married man."
A telegram from early October 1918 made clear the charge against him: "Strictly confidential...it is rumored that Capt. Nangle C.F. has become a married man...confidentially ascertain and report by telegraph whether any truth in rumor and whether he is still a Roman Catholic Chaplain..."

In early November, Newfoundland's Minister of Militia wrote to Archbishop Roche indicating that the rumors about Father Nangle had been fully investigated and found to be false. The archbishop replied on November 2, saying he was "glad at last to have an official denial of the absurd report."

The principal Roman Roman Catholic chaplain of the British Army, The Right Rev. Bishop Keating, C.M.G., C.F. had also "made careful enquiries regarding the statements made in connection with the Rev. T. Nangle, C.F. and is satisfied that those statements are incorrect."

On October 20, the Regiment was thrown into the fray yet again when it was part of an advance near Harlebeke. "By this time the Battalion strength of the Royal Newfoundland Regiment was a mere 256 men, a quarter of a full battalion's strength," says Christie.

On October 25, 1918, the Regiment was in its last fight of the war near Ooteghem. They met with heavy German fire and in one day lost 19 men. On October 26, the Royal Newfoundland Regiment was withdrawn from the Front for good. The Battalion was in Kuurne when the Armistice was announced. The First World War raged for four years, three months and 14 days, ending with the signing of an Armistice on November 11, 1918. That day, *The Evening Telegram* in St. John's ran a huge headline: "Germany has surrendered. The war ended at 11 o'clock this morning, Paris time."

At the time of the Armistice, Hagerty says there were 649 Roman Catholic chaplains serving out of a total of 3,475 British Expeditionary Force chaplains. According to Christie, of the "4,253 soldiers of the Royal Newfoundland Regiment who served in France and Belgium, 1,152 died." This was a fatality rate of 27 percent, the highest on the Western Front.

The Royal Newfoundland Regiment had distinguished itself in action on many occasions and won a reputation for bravery, dogged determination and courage under fire. But this sterling reputation was paid for in the blood of the dead, the scars of the wounded and the weakened minds of the "shell-shocked." And, though the war had ended, the work of Father Tom Nangle was really just beginning.

~ CHAPTER NINE ~

WAR GRAVES COMMISSION

To commemorate the service and sacrifice of the Royal Newfoundland Regiment in WWI, a series of caribou stamps were issued on January 2, 1919. According to researcher Thomas Nemec, there were stamps with twelve values in the series ranging from one to thirty-six cents. All the stamps show the head of a large stag caribou, and eight of the twelve values carry the inscription "Trail of the Caribou" below the stag's head. Nemec says this phrase "was proposed by LCol. Thomas Nangle, the Roman Catholic chaplain of the Regiment."

Following the Armistice, the war-torn nations of Europe began the long process of rebuilding. Part of the post-war reconstruction involved the creation of military cemeteries to honour the fallen. The scattered war dead were gathered, where possible identified, and then buried in neatly arranged military cemeteries.

In Britain, an Imperial War Graves Commission (IWGC) was established with the task of overseeing the establishment, creation and maintenance of military graveyards. Initially, this was a National (British) Committee but on the suggestion of the Prince of Wales it included all parts of the British Empire which had fought for the King, including Australia, Canada, New Zealand, South Africa and Newfoundland. Today, this organization is known as the Commonwealth War Graves Commission.

The IWGC was chartered to construct and decorate the military cemeteries in proper fashion, and mark each grave as "permanently as man's art can devise," and also to deal with the various European nations in which Imperial troops had fallen and been buried.

The Commonwealth War Graves Commission was established by Royal Charter of May 21, 1917, the provisions of which were amended and extended by a Supplemental Charter of June 8, 1964. Its duties are to mark and maintain the graves of members of the forces of the Commonwealth who died in the two world wars, to build and maintain memorials to the dead whose graves are unknown, and to keep records and registers. The cost is shared by partner governments: Australia, Canada, India, New Zealand and South Africa, in proportions based on the numbers of their graves.

In the aftermath of the war, Father Nangle returned to his priestly duties in the parish of St. Michael's on Bell Island where he worked for four months, according to the records of the Roman Roman Catholic Archives in St. John's.

In March, 1919, a story appeared in *The Newfoundland Magazine* which heaped praise on Nangle's war service:

> *The Reverend Thomas Nangle has been to the very gates of hell on earth which we call war. He has been in the thick of it, often, as Governor Davidson put it, 'repeatedly working under fire, regardless of instructions that he should keep out of it. Of such stuff Nangle was made. The broad minded spirit of the man raised him above petty sectarianism and he bestowed praise alike on men of all denominations.*

But being a parish priest was not in Father Tom Nangle's future. He was selected as the Dominion of Newfoundland's representative to the IWGC. He was also appointed Director of Graves Registration and Enquiry by the Government of Newfoundland.

In this capacity, he took on two primary roles. First, was the collection, identification and re-burial of Newfoundlanders killed and hastily buried in action. Second, was the creation of a series of permanent monuments to the valour and sacrifice of the Royal Newfoundland Regiment in WWI.

While Father Nangle was getting involved in commemorating the colony's fallen, the winds of political change was underway in Newfoundland. O'Flaherty says in April 1919 the government announced plans to hold an election in May. This set off a series of protests at the timing of the snap-election call, including ex-servicemen meeting to discuss forming their own political party. According to O'Flaherty, the veterans decided against creating a political party but the idea would come up again in 1924 and at that time Padre Nangle would be involved.

On July 24, 1919, Nangle was given his marching orders to travel to Europe and begin the gruesome task of locating and identifying the scattered war dead, and re-burying them in organized military cemeteries:

To: Capt. T. Nangle, C. F.

> *You have been detailed to proceed to France and Belgium for the purpose of registering and collecting the isolated bodies of Newfoundland soldiers into military cemeteries....*
> *You will proceed to London via Liverpool by S.S. "Sachem" and report at the Pay and Record Office, London on arrival.*
>
> *In addition to the work of registering these graves and having the bodies collected, you will also endeavour to arrange with the Imperial War Graves Commission and, if necessary, with the French Authorities for the erection of a permanent monument at such places as Beaumont Hamel. But before*

proceeding with such work you will please inform this office....of the likely cost of the purchase and erection of such a Memorial. You will report progress periodically to the Pay and Records Office, London, who will have been instructed to transmit such information to this Office.

It is hoped that with your personal knowledge of the location of the graves, and with the help of Private Snow, that all isolated bodies of Newfoundland soldiers will eventually be collected.

                              Lieut. Col.
                              Chief Staff Officer

Private Henry Snow had been a stretcher-bearer with the Royal Newfoundland Regiment during the war, and it was thought his knowledge of battlefield burials would assist Father Nangle in completing his work.

During battles, men were sometimes buried where they fell, perhaps in a ditch, or by a roadside. In some cases men were not buried, but simply left where they fell.

Now the wish of the Government of Newfoundland was to have these bodies collected, identified and re-interred in dignified military cemeteries being constructed in Gallipoli, Belgium and France.

Nangle was "authorised to incur the necessary expenditure in order to have this work satisfactorily carried out." His costs were to be borne by the Newfoundland Government. In fulfilling his duties, he was seconded from the Chaplain General's Department and reattached to the Royal Newfoundland Regiment. He would later write that he was sent to Europe by Prime Minister Michael Cashin on the recommendation of Colonel Bernard.

The same month he was given his orders to proceed to Europe, Nangle's military rank was raised from Captain to Acting Major. Along with this promotion came an increase in power, pay and influence.

Private Snow, the stretcher-bearer who carried so many of the wounded and dying during the war and who was to accompany Nangle to Europe, was promoted to Acting Sergeant.

When Nangle arrived in Europe, he presented himself to Major General Fabian Ware, the Director General of Graves' Registration and Enquiry. He reported Ware "has given me every assistance and help in the carrying out of my duties."

In a letter to the Pay and Records office dated August 20, 1919, Major Nangle requested a per diem of $10 for himself, and $2 for Sergeant Snow while in France.

By this time, he was realizing the immense proportions of the task with which he was charged. He wrote to his superiors indicating his work might take longer than initially thought.

In late August 1919, Archbishop Roche wrote to Nangle saying he would like to take a tour of the Front the following year as part of a trip to Rome. Roche also said he was "enclosing the celebrat for one year." The celebrat, according to archivist Larry Dohey, was a letter from the Archbishop testifying that Father Nangle was free from canonical censure and therefore should be permitted to make the Holy Sacrifice of Mass in whatever diocese he might find himself.

By mid-September 1919, Father Nangle had completed a "Preliminary Report on War Graves and Battle Exploit Memorials." He explained that he had divided Newfoundland's war graves into five sectors: United Kingdom; Gallipoli; France and Belgium; prisoners of war; Newfoundland.

He recommended the Newfoundland government should erect six memorial sites that would mark the critical battles fought by the Newfoundland Regiment: Caribou Hill at Gallipoli; Beaumont Hamel, Gueudecourt, Monchy-le-Preux and Marcoing in France; and Keiberg Ridge in Belgium. These sites were also accepted by the Battle Exploits Memorial Committee. Nangle referred to these memorial sites as the "Trail of the Caribou." We were unable to discover why Nangle's recommendation to build a caribou memorial at Gallipoli never came to fruition. Caribou Hill was where the Regiment won its first WW1 decorations, and Gallipoli was where the Regiment received its "baptism of fire."

In the United Kingdom alone there were graves of Newfoundland soldiers in 19 places. "Those scattered graves stand as monuments to blaze the 'Trail of the Caribou' through the Mother Country," Nangle wrote. The graves in the U.K. were those of soldiers who died in English hospitals of wounds suffered in action. Wandsworth, for instance, boasts both a military hospital and a graveyard where a number of Newfoundlanders are buried.

As scattered as some of these English graveyards were, the graves of Newfoundland's fallen were not totally forgotten. An American delegation from the Knights of Columbus visited the graves of its members in Winchester on May 30, 1919 and laid wreaths on the graves of the resting Newfoundlanders.

Nangle recommended a central stone cross be erected in each of the nineteen cemeteries, in addition to the Regimental headstone. He estimated the cost at about £100 sterling.

In regards to the 43 Newfoundland graves at Gallipoli, Nangle said he had recently interviewed an officer who had been investigating the condition of the Australian graves and was told that the Newfoundland graves were in very bad condition.

Nangle commented extensively on the Newfoundlanders buried in France and Belgium. He wrote:

> *I have just returned from a preliminary visit to France and Belgium. I was accompanied by the Hon. R.K. Bishop and Capt. Anderson, M.B.E., so that they, on their return to Newfoundland may be able to give you some idea of the work done by the Directorate of Graves' Registration and Enquiries. I am very glad I had them with me because it is impossible for anyone who has not seen the battlefields to realize the work required. The task in hand has been greatly augmented by subsequent fighting over our battlefields, the healing forces of nature having made it impossible to recognize old landmarks - not to speak of isolated unmarked graves...Monchy is about the worst sight in the whole line. It was No Man's Land from April '17 until the end. I hope to begin my task of searching the battlefields here in a week or ten days but I am afraid the task is hopeless and that very few identifications will be made...Next I visited Gueudecourt and as nearly three years have elapsed since we fought over the ground, the prospect of identifying bodies is next to impossible. The last place I visited was Beaumont Hamel. Here all the bodies have been collected into cemeteries and any that have not will never be found.*

In this section of his report, he hinted at what problems were confounding his work. Battlefields had been fought over relentlessly. Trenches had been blown in by heavy artillery bombardments. At the same time, the erosive effects of three years of rain and wind, not too mention regrowth of bushes, shrubs, small trees and other vegetation had changed the landscape.

Some of the Newfoundlanders had been buried where they fell in villages, on farms, along roads, railway lines and streets. After the war, the population of France and Belgium had quickly begun to rebuild and return to as normal a pace of life as possible. Reconstruction entombed many isolated graves meaning that some men would never be re-interred in proper military cemeteries.

One significant point Nangle made in this report was that given the immense number of dead (more than 500,000 British dead in France alone) the removal of bodies to England for re-burial would be impossible. He went on to say:

> *In due time, therefore, wherever a man may be buried, from Newfoundland to Gallipoli, his grave will be marked in the same manner as the rest of his comrades, officers and men alike.*

Tom Nangle's son, Hugh, recalls his father talking about the work of scouring the battlefields of France and Belgium for the scattered graves of Newfoundland's sons:

> *I remember his comments about the work for the War Graves Commission, that people had no idea how hard this work was, trying to identify the corpses. The dead were often in a gelatinous state, decay had begun. Father said it was more of a shock than having to give the Last Rites to a dying man. It was just horrific work.*

Hugh said his father described the searching for bodies, exhumation of graves and process of trying to identify corpses as "hard, hard grinding work, that at times was very dispiriting."

> *It was awful to disinter people and go through the process of trying to identify them. There were so many who couldn't be identified. He said that the mass graves were a curse. And, he felt it was remarkable that so few workman didn't become severely ill from dealing with the bodies in decay.*

The workmen wore no face masks, breathing apparatus, goggles or other protective gear. Often teams of soldiers simply wore their uniforms and used bare hands to search with shovels for the remains of the fallen. Hugh has vivid memories of his father talking about the terrible smell that hung over the exhumed graves:

> *He said the smell was appalling. After a day's work he'd get a bath but the smell of rotting flesh would remain in his mouth and nose. But he believed it was essential work to be done. However, quite a few who did the work of exhuming graves were effected psychologically by it and were turned off and quit after just 3 or 4 weeks.*

Missing in Action

Another important aspect of Father Tom Nangle's work was how to best commemorate the huge number of men missing in action. According to Christie, "Half of those killed (250,000 men) fighting on the Western Front are missing and have no known grave."

Christie noted as well that of the 1,201 members of the Royal Newfoundland Regiment killed in action, 591 have no known grave.

Nangle recommended that "mural tablets be erected to each (missing) man in the nearest cemetery." Eventually, however, the Government of Newfoundland decided to remember all of its missing soldiers, sailors, and merchant marine on tablets to be placed at Beaumont Hamel.

Father Nangle was a Newfoundlander through and through, so it's not surprising that he asked in his report:

> *Do you think it feasible to have our Regimental Headstones made in Newfoundland of native granite or other stone? This*

> would be distinctive and easily recognized in large cemeteries.... Moreover, it will give parents in Newfoundland an opportunity of seeing their sons' headstone, who otherwise may never have the opportunity of doing so.

He was concerned about the families of the fallen. He wanted to try and give them a chance to at least see the headstones of their fallen sons, brothers, cousins and nephews. He knew that many people would never get a chance to travel to Europe and visit the grave sites.

His report next discussed the issue of erecting "Battle Exploit Memorials" to the Regiment. He said a military committee had been established to examine the claims to sites made by various Armies, Divisions, Regiments and Dominions in different campaigns and battles.

Newfoundland was not represented on this committee and therefore he said he had to ask to have the deadline of September 1st extended so that the Dominion could make its claims to areas for the erection of battle memorials.

He pointed out that the 12th Division had laid claim to Monchy-le-Preux for the erection of a battle memorial, and asked that the site be given to Newfoundland. General Ware apparently supported his claim.

Of the proposed monuments, Nangle used very strong words to argue that no expense should be spared to remember the fallen:

> They are monuments to our glorious dead, and to our just as glorious survivors. They are monuments to the mothers that bore such brave sons and the land that bred them. They are to be an everlasting tribute to the men who gave their all that the land may live. Surely then if St. John's could erect an expensive temporary arch for a two days' celebration,

> *Newfoundland can spend more than 100 pounds per monument to commemorate in perpetuity the doings of her Regiment, and her 1,200 dead. If 100 pounds is all that can be spared per monument...I recommend that we erect nothing at all. Let us forget we ever had a Regiment.*

Padre Nangle was clearly fired up. He wanted to see a fitting series of memorials to the Regiment and the men buried there.

In his report on graves and memorials, he suggested that a committee of "energetic citizens be formed and a public subscription list opened; the amount raised to be doubled by the Government." This was Nangle's first foray into public fund-raising, but it wouldn't be his last.

He said "anything less than £1,000 in France per monument would be unworthy, as would anything less than £100 for each of our main cemeteries in the U.K."

He recommended a figure of approximately £6,400, or about $35,000, was necessary in order to erect four monuments in France, one each in Gallipoli and Belgium, and smaller monuments at four military cemeteries in the United Kingdom: Wandsworth, Brookwood, Ayr and Winchester.

With this final suggestion, he ended his "Preliminary Report on War Graves and Battle Exploit Memorials."

In later years, he would tell his son, Hugh, that Gallipoli was seen primarily as an Anzac (Australia-New Zealand Army Corps) battlefield and it was almost as though Newfoundland had never been there. He wanted to ensure the sacrifice of the Newfoundland Regiment in the Dardanelles was not forgotten and that was why he specified a monument at Gallipoli.

Hugh said his father often talked about his work in creating the battlefield memorials to the fallen of the Royal Newfoundland Regiment:

> *He said it was part of his commitment to the mothers and sisters of Newfoundland. This was a point he made again and again. Dad had enormous admiration for the women of Newfoundland. He said they were the backbone of the country...Dad felt there was a heavy duty on his conscience (to remember the fallen) because many had died as a result of his recruiting work. A lot of the men had responded to his recruitment efforts...*

Hugh thinks part of what drove his father to work on creating the "Trail of the Caribou" in Europe was because he felt so strongly about the huge loss of life his country had suffered, and especially the impact of this loss on families left behind.

Hugh believes his father's almost vehement attitude in working on the battlefield memorials for the Regiment was also driven by the enormous number of men who were missing, the men blown to pieces during battle, or those who lay in unmarked graves in the mud of a roadside ditch:

> *Father was mortified by the loss of life....Harder still was exhuming and trying to identify individuals and re-burying them. Realizing that so many weren't identified or were missing devastated father. It was almost as though each body identified was a victory and those who weren't were an enormous loss for him, a defeat.*

Father Tom Nangle was engulfed in his work, and determined to ensure the "Trail of the Caribou" was clearly marked.

~ Chapter Ten ~

CARIBOU MEMORIALS

The Royal Newfoundland Regiment's badges were adorned with the head of a mighty stag caribou. Unlike the moose which was introduced to the island of Newfoundland, the caribou Rangifer was a native mammal.

If cod was the currency of Newfoundland in the late 19th and early 20th centuries, caribou was king. Famous sportsmen from all over the world made the trek to Newfoundland's barren interior in search of a trophy stag. A large male caribou is a visually stunning animal, powerful, magnificent and proud with high, long antlers. It is a noble monarch of the rocky Gaff Topsails in Newfoundland's barren interior. Given the historical and cultural link between the Regiment and its native symbol, it was to become a poignant sign of the Dominion of Newfoundland's sacrifices in World War One. In Gallipoli, where the Regiment first saw action during the First World War, a hill is named "Caribou Hill" in their honour.

Nangle on the Trail of the Caribou:

In a letter marked "urgent" and dated October 6, 1919, Nangle wrote to the Minister of Militia in St. John's requesting a copy of the photo of "The Monarch of the Topsails" and "half a dozen photos of caribou in various positions for use by the artist in designing the battle exploit memorials."

"The Monarch of the Topsails" was a caption first used by well known Newfoundland photographer S.H. Parsons for a picture he took on the West Coast of Newfoundland in about 1900 when he accompanied a survey crew with the Reid Newfoundland Railway Company. The "Monarch" was a large stag caribou with its head thrown back and nose defiantly thrust into the air, bugling its defiance.

Second Report on War Graves

By October 1919, Nangle had completed a "Second Report on War Graves and Battle Exploit Memorials." Addressing the Minister of Militia, he said rapid progress had been made since his last report. He said a meeting had been held on September 30, 1919, at the Adjutant General's office and "among other things our claims to memorials were discussed."

He said he had received sixteen designs for memorials and monuments, some of which were "good, others very bad."

> *I have got in touch with Capt. (Basil) Gotto the gentleman who designed "The Bombing Newfoundlander" [in Bowring Park, St. John's] which won a place in this Year's Academy. Capt. Gotto is very enthusiastic in everything concerning Newfoundland, having coming in contact with our men while Staff Officer at Winchester. He has been well known in British Art for the past thirty years.*

> *His proposition is much cheaper than any of the others, it will be artistic and from what I have seen of those already erected in France will be most distinctive, his idea being a giant caribou somewhat like the "Monarch of the Topsails" carved in bronze on a rough cairn of Newfoundland granite about ten to fifteen feet high. This will be distinctive of the Regiment and of Newfoundland. It will be artistic....I urge you to get the Government to adopt this idea as it will be one of the best monuments in France and worthy of the Royal Newfoundland Regiment.*

Padre Nangle had set the wheels in motion for the creation of the five European Caribou Memorials. Four would be in France (Beaumont Hamel, Gueudecourt, Monchy le Preux and Masnieres) and one in Belgium (Courtrai). Today, most Newfoundlanders, even those who have not been to the five Memorials in France and Belgium, are aware that a caribou statue marks the sacrifices of the Newfoundland Regiment in Europe.

In an article in *The Veteran* magazine in 1921, Captain H.A. Anderson wrote that "the origin of the caribou (memorials) must be credited to LCol. Nangle through whose efforts the idea materialized." It was Nangle who coined the term "Trail of the Caribou" when he used it as the title for his address at the Casino Theatre in St. John's in 1917.

Later in life, Tom Nangle would praise the work of artist Basil Gotto to his son. Hugh remembers his father saying he was lucky Gotto was such a fine craftsman:

> *Dad was very careful to ensure that I understood it wasn't a one-man band. It was a team effort, not only in France and Belgium and Gallipoli, but in Newfoundland. There were others who mucked in and made sure things were done. Two politicians were influential, Dad said, Prime Minister Sir Richard Squires and Governor Davidson. William Coaker (head of the Fishermen's Protective Union) was also enormously influential in helping Father to get to see people, open doors or helping in many ways.*

In the photo section, the reader will find pictures of Prime Minister Squires and Sir William Ford Coaker, both of whom visited Europe and walked the blood-soaked battlefields with Nangle. Not only was Nangle doing the morally "right" thing in appropriately remembering the war dead, but he had the political will of the government and high profile personalities behind him.

Nangle had traveled much of the "Trail of the Caribou" during his tenure as chaplain to the Royal Newfoundland Regiment. Now he was working to ensure that trail would be marked for perpetuity, so that the sacrifices of men who hailed from a tiny country in the New World would not be forgotten.

Nangle's report to Newfoundland's Minister of Militia discussed his work in locating, exhuming and identifying the graves of Newfoundlanders, accompanied by Sergeants H. Snow and J. Murphy:

> *Whenever one of our graves was found it was tidied, a cross erected and if possible photographed, copies of these photographs will be sent to you for your distribution to the next-of-kin. When the bodies have been interred in proper military cemeteries and the IWGC headstone erected they will be photographed again.*

Just as when he asked to have tombstones made in Newfoundland, Nangle was concerned with sending pictures of graves home for families. Realizing many families would never get the opportunity to visit France, Belgium, Gallipoli or cemeteries in the United Kingdom he tired to provide some level of comfort in showing them the final resting place of the Regiment's dead. In the coming months, he tried to organize a trip for families of Newfoundland soldiers to visit the graveyards of Europe.

His report mentioned the difficulty in marking graves:

> *To give you some idea of how the landscape has been battered it took me one whole day to find a quarry 35 feet deep from which I could find my way to Sgt. Ash's grave.*

Of the Gueudecourt area, he said, "this whole area is a forest of little white wooden crosses bearing the inscription 'Unknown British Soldier.'"

His report also explained that there would be space on each headstone for a personal inscription by the family. The space was limited to sixty-six letters at a cost of about seven cents per letter. Once again, we see his efforts to involve the families of the fallen in the creation of their loved one's final resting place. We can speculate he hoped to give some level of comfort to families by letting them add a personal inscription.

Another of Father Nangle's chores in this period involved negotiations to gain control of the actual land where the memorials were to be located. He had conducted interviews with the French and Belgian governments regarding the sites for the battlefield memorials. In a letter addressed to the Chief Staff Officer of the Newfoundland Contingent dated November 4, 1919, Nangle was advised that the price of the land at Gueudecourt was 1,650 francs for about one acre, or 4,100 meters square.

In Beaumont Hamel, he was forced to negotiate with approximately 250 French farmers for the land on which to develop a memorial park. He said this "took considerable time and work as the owners had been dispersed by the war and were now residing in various places from Dunkirk to Morocco." One landowner refused to sell because he believed a rich mineral find had been made. But after nearly three years of holding out, the individual relented when he realized Nangle's true intentions.

It is worth noting that, while the Government of Newfoundland purchased the land, under French law there are problems with foreign governments owning land in France. As such, the Beaumont-Hamel Memorial was included, along with other sites in the same situation, in the Convention dated December 18, 1938 which was entered between the French Government and the governments of the United Kingdom, Canada, Australia and New Zealand. It was agreed that the sites listed, previously acquired as specified, would be vested in the French state but would then be granted to the governments concerned or to the Commonwealth War Graves Commission upon the terms stipulated. Beaumont-Hamel was granted free of charge and in perpetuity to the Government of Newfoundland while it remains "exclusively appropriated to the purpose of the commemorative monument." Following Newfoundland's entry into Canadian Confederation, Beaumont-Hamel and the other Newfoundland memorials became the responsibility of Canada.

Father Tom Nangle's good work was not going unnoticed. On November 14, 1919, Newfoundland's Minister of Militia wrote a letter commending him to the Chief Staff Officer at the Pay and Records office at 58 Victoria Street London, England. In that letter the minister said: "I understand that Major Nangle has been doing very excellent work since his arrival and his efforts are appreciated."

~ CHAPTER ELEVEN ~

PLANNING THE MEMORIALS

In December 1919, Nangle returned to St. John's where he gave a full report of his work in Europe to Prime Minister Richard Squires.

In a letter to the Chief Staff Officer of the Newfoundland Contingent dated January 2, 1920, the Minister of Militia for Newfoundland said "it is the wish of the Government that Major Nangle should (continue to) represent them in connection with the work of the Battle Exploits Memorial, Graves, Cemeteries, etc."

The letter said Nangle was sailing for England on January 3rd aboard S.S. Sachem and asked that he be supplied with a clerk to help him run his office when he was scouring the battlefields.

The letter also noted that Nangle was preparing to visit Gallipoli and asked if a man who knew that area could travel with him. The Minister of Militia said it was Government's intention to erect a memorial on the site known as "Caribou Hill."

On January 3rd Nangle telegraphed sculptor Capt. Basil Gotto, and the message was short and sweet: "Government approves model proceed immediately."

The Government of Newfoundland had approved Gotto's memorial design of a magnificent stag caribou bugling. Father Tom Nangle's work was beginning to bear fruit.

That same day, Nangle sent a telegram to General McNulty of the Chaplain General's Office. In it, he said he was returning immediately to identify graves in Cambrai area. In addition to developing a series of battle exploits memorials to the Royal Newfoundland Regiment, he was still undertaking his gruesome work of exhuming, identifying and re-interring soldiers killed in action.

On January 6, 1920, Deputy Colonial Secretary Arthur Mews wrote the minutes of the Executive Council, stating that:

> *The design submitted by Basil Gotto for War Memorial in the form of mound with Caribou in bronze is approved. Memorials to be erected at Beaumont Hamel, Gueudecourt, Marcoing, Monchy le Preux and Keiberg Ridge....Monuments to be erected at Gallipoli, Rockwood, Ayr and Winchester....Major Nangle is authorized to act on behalf of the Newfoundland Government in all matters pertaining to the graves of deceased Newfoundland soldiers and sailors in the British Isles, Europe and Gallipoli and the erection of memorials and monuments.*

In February, Sir William Coaker was in France and met with Nangle. Together they toured battlefields, visited graves and viewed prospective memorial sites. One of the sites they visited was the prospective memorial park at Beaumont Hamel. Coaker also visited the grave of his nephew, Christian, who had fallen in combat.

In the photo section the reader will see pictures of Coaker and Nangle on their tours. A very influential politician and leader of the powerful Fishermen's Protective Union, Coaker was very supportive of Nangle's work. In 1924 he wrote:

> *Before passing on, I must place on record my deep appreciation of the splendid work of...Nangle. He is well chosen for this sacred duty of caring for our dead in France and Flanders. He has done splendid work at Beaumont Hamel. My hope is that he will be permitted to finish that good work...*

On March 3, 1920, Coaker sent a telegram to Prime Minister Squires:

> *Recommend authorize Nangle purchase field Beaumont Hamel to value of Ten Thousand Dollars....Communicate Nangle immediately as necessary to secure property in original condition before working parties fill trenches etc. Also authorize Nangle employ men concentrate all bodies around Beaumont Hamel in proposed purchase where memorial will be erected. Matter urgent.*

Later that same day, Squires responded to Coaker, saying that Nangle had been granted full authority to secure the best possible site for the Beaumont Hamel Memorial. Squires told Coaker he would cable Nangle confirming his instructions regarding Beaumont Hamel. He wrote:

> *Have just received cable from Coaker concerning Beaumont Hamel purchase. When you were here Government authorized you to make this purchase...Any special authority you require for the purchase of Beaumont Hamel field at cost of ten thousand dollars and the concentration of bodies around Beaumont Hamel is hereby given. I regard your work as very important and am depending upon you to do the very best possible for the honour of our heroic dead and perpetuation the remembrance of Royal Newfoundland Regiment and Royal Naval Reserve.*

The significance of Nangle's work was understood and appreciated by both Coaker and Squires. Prime Minister Squires, his wife Helena, and their daughter would eventually visit Europe and tour sites with Father Nangle, as Coaker had done.

In a 1926 article for *The Veteran* magazine, Nangle said it was Coaker's idea to buy the whole field at Beaumont Hamel after he was briefed on the graves in the area.

Coaker was very impressed by Nangle. On March 8, 1920, he wired Prime Minister Squires from London and suggested that Major Nangle be promoted to LCol. to "give him standing in performance of his duties in France."

One has to try and imagine the immense quantity of work that Father Nangle was completing at this time. He was a relentless, dynamic individual and many who knew him wrote of his tireless enthusiasm. He was scouring battlefields for graves, identifying corpses (where possible) and re-interring bodies in proper military cemeteries. Travel and communication in the early twentieth century was not what it is today, and this must have slowed his efforts.

At the same time, he was negotiating with various levels of government in France, Belgium and at Gallipoli for plots of land to construct and erect memorials and monuments. He was involved as well with various politicians from Newfoundland who were interested in seeing his work, touring and inspecting these sites.

He was also undoubtedly feeling pressure from the families of the dead soldiers of the Regiment. It was now two years since the war had ended and the erection of memorials and creation of military cemeteries was proceeding at a snail's pace.

Nangle was responsible for the 19 graveyards in the United Kingdom where Newfoundlanders who died of their wounds in British military hospitals were buried. On May 25th, Prime Minister Squires cabled Father Nangle and requested an update on the cemetery near Wandsworth Military Hospital in England. Apparently there was some controversy over this site between the Imperial War Graves Commission and the Newfoundland War Contingent Association (NWCA). As if Tom Nangle didn't have enough on his plate, Sir Richard Squires demanded answers from him.

By mid-June 1920, Nangle had completed his third report as Director of Graves Registration and Enquiries. This was a special report on Wandsworth cemetery and the controversy brewing there.

At the center of the dispute was the fact that the NWCA wanted to erect a memorial in the graveyard at cost of £400. Nangle wrote that this idea would be fine if all the deceased members of the Regiment buried in the United Kingdom were interred at Wandsworth. However, the soldiers were buried in more than a dozen military cemeteries, and the Newfoundland government could not be expected to spend £400 on each of these sites.

More important than the monetary issue was the idea of treating some of the Regiment's fallen differently than others. Nangle said the spirit of the Regiment and the spirit of the IWGC was that "officers and men, no matter in what part of the world they lie, should be treated in the same manner." He didn't want to see a large cenotaph erected in Wandsworth Cemetery and have smaller monument crosses in the other cemeteries in the United Kingdom, Europe and Gallipoli. Nangle, and the IWGC, wanted to treat all fallen soldiers as equals, regardless of rank, religion or civilian social status. This incident also hints at a part of Tom Nangle's character that was more evident in the coming years. He was not afraid to speak his mind and call things as he saw them. He sometimes spoke from the heart with little regard for consequences.

Nangle concluded his third report with some comments which hinted at the mounting pressure being directed at the speed of his work:

> *Your Government and the relatives of our fallen soldiers may rest assured that everything possible is being done as speedily and as thoroughly as possible, considering the gigantic size and the slow movements of such a huge organization as the Imperial War Graves Commission.*

Historian Norm Christie says in the 1920s there was a severe shortage of qualified labour in France, and Nangle's early efforts at constructing the Battle Exploit Memorials fell dismally behind schedule. As European countries struggled to rebuild after the terrible destruction of warfare, tradesmen of all sorts were all in heavy demand, and this would surely have impacted on Nangle's efforts to build the memorials and monuments.

Despite the slow pace of the construction of the memorials, and the controversy surrounding Wandsworth Cemetery, Nangle's promotion to LCol., which Sir William Coaker had recommended, was finally gazetted in December 1920.

That same month, Prime Minister Squires met with Governor Charles Alexander Harris and asked that LCol. Nangle be officially commended to the King for his work with the IWGC. Harris succeeded Nangle's friend and confidant, Walter Davidson, as governor in late 1917 and remained in the post for five years. Harris would downplay the achievements of Father Tom Nangle by refusing to recommend him for important honours.

Squires urged Governor Harris to recommend Nangle be appointed a "Companion of the Order of St. Michael and St.

George," or C.M.G. In a confidential dispatch to the Viscount Milner in London, Harris discussed Sir Richard Squires' wish for Nangle to have the C.M.G. conferred upon him.

Sadly, the dispatch reveals that the Governor did not share Squires' enthusiasm for conferring such an honour upon Nangle. Harris said he felt it would be more suitable for Nangle to be made a "Commander of the Order of the British Empire" (C.B.E.) but only "if the matter were pressed."

Harris went on to write that "this honour is asked not so much as a matter of desert as in order to gratify the claims of Newfoundland as a Colony and it is open to question upon that ground."

The governor concluded by reiterating that the military C.B.E would be a more suitable award for LCol. Nangle than the C.M.G.

~ CHAPTER TWELVE ~

NEWFOUNDLAND'S WAR MEMORIALS

In early 1921, LCol. Tom Nangle was as busy as ever. But not too busy to collect some war memorabilia for the Newfoundland Museum in St. John's. In a January 6, 1921 letter to museum curator H. Shortis he wrote about a German anti-tank rifle he had collected. He compared the German weapon to sealing guns of outport Newfoundland:

> I think it will put your mind on the 'Long Toms' as used by the old-time sealers. With a half dozen fingers (of powder) and a good big slug, I think it would prove a very formidable weapon.

Hugh Nangle remembers when he was growing up in Rhodesia his father was very much against the idea of sport hunting and guns in general. Hugh said when his older brother, Timothy Haig Nangle, reached adolescence and wanted to own a rifle for hunting his father was very, very reluctant to let him have one. "Dad had seen enough of guns for a lifetime," Hugh says.

On January 11, 1921, Father Nangle wrote the Colonial Secretary of Newfoundland regarding the official seal of the island colony. Continuing with his work of commemorating the actions of the Royal Newfoundland Regiment, he said he intended to have flags made for the various cathedrals in France in which tablets to the memory of the Regiment were to be placed.

On February 16, 1921, Nangle again wrote to museum curator Shortis, saying:

> *It was very gratifying to me to know that the tank rifle I sent you was suitable for the Museum and appreciated by you. From time to time if I find things worth while I shall forward them to you, but I am afraid it is to late now to start collecting; that should have been two yeas ago....As a boy I remember seeing trucks of old French cannons on my grand-mother's property on the South Side (of St. John's harbor), whether they are there yet or not I do not know. It is a great pity that these things were not preserved, but I am afraid that in a hundred years time people will be saying the same thing about our generation.*

This letter again gives insight into Nangle's character. He was a man concerned with recording and preserving history. He had an interest in commemorating history so that future generations might understand what had happened.

On March 17, 1921, Nangle sent a letter to the Committee of Imperial Defence in London enquiring about the precise start and end dates of the Battle of the Somme. He was concerned about having the correct dates for the inscription on memorial tablets.

On March 22, 1921, Governor Harris of Newfoundland wrote to Colonial Secretary Winston Churchill regarding the conferring of Royal honours on the King's birthday. One of the cases he mentioned was that of LCol. Nangle, whom Prime Minister Squires had again recommended for the prestigious C.M.G.

The Prime Minister had begun by once again urging the case

of Lieutenant Colonel Father Nangle. He strongly pressed him for a C.M.G. and endeavoured to compare his merits favourably with those of Dr. MacPherson who received a C.M.G. for his war service. "But I am afraid that I cannot myself support the recommendation with any warmth, and I know that in some quarters it would be very unpopular. I cannot think that this case is one of special strength," said Harris.

While Squires was firmly behind Nangle and his work, it is quite apparent the Governor was not as enthusiastic.

The Public War Memorial

In June of 1921, the issue of a war memorial came to a head in St. John's when Philip E. Outerbridge called a public meeting to discuss the matter. Outerbridge was a director of Harvey and Company. He was elected to St. John's City Council in the municipal election of December 15, 1921.

The Public War Memorial meeting was held at the Board of Trade Building on June 9 and chaired by Mr. H. Cowan, President of the Board. In attendance were about 90 people including Sir P.T. McGrath, Dr. Curtis, Mr. George Ayre, Mr. R.G. Rendell (OBE), Mr. John Higgins (President of the GWVA), Lady [Mitchie Ann] Crosbie, Mrs. W.J. Herder and Lady Reid, a veritable who's who of St. John's society of the time.

Outerbridge was of the opinion that no further delay should take place in the erection of a war memorial. After debate and discussion, a War Memorial Committee was established with Rendell as Chair and Outerbridge as Secretary-Treasurer. They were empowered to select an executive. All present agreed in taking immediate action for the collection of funds for a public war memorial.

On June 16, 1921, the first meeting of the executive of the War Memorial Committee was held. Lady Crosbie strongly favored the immediate launching of the War Memorial Company Unlimited and the public selling of shares in that company. Mrs. Keegan moved, Lady Crosbie seconded that the cost of these shares be one dollar. Other methods of raising money to be employed included: voluntary subscription, canvassing of St. John's and outports, and a special collection in all churches.

The War Memorial Committee met on July 4th, and by that time had raised $8,699.94. But the committee had reconsidered the idea of a house-to-house canvass, and at a meeting on July 14th they decided to abandon the idea of going door-to-door because it was deemed inappropriate.

On August 9, 1921, the committee met and the main topic of discussion was eight possible sites for the monument. These sites included: Harvey Road near the Newfoundland Constabulary Inspector General's residence; opposite the Roman Catholic Palace Gate; the top of Court House Hill; the Beach; Ordnance Street Park; Park adjacent to Methodist Church; Bannerman Park near the bandstand; Bannerman Park near Military Road.

Two weeks later, on August 16, the committee reconvened and the importance of choosing a site for the monument was debated. Lady Crosbie pressed for the selection of the King's Beach [Water Street] site. Mr. Bradshaw expressed the concern that a site be finalized before estimates could be received from architects. But about a month later, on September 12, the committee still could not decide on the precise location the monument should be placed.

By early October, the Monument Committee met and apart from the difficulty in selecting a site, it was now apparent that fund-raising had stalled. While some monies were still trickling in, including a donation of $148 from the employees of Ayre and Sons, and $63 from the workers of the Royal Stores, the committee's bank balance was basically at a stand-still. Lawyer and former MHA William R. Howley, who later became a judge, felt that "the fact that the erection of the memorial was being delayed through lack of financial support should be conveyed to the relatives of those who had died."

Nangle

It is unclear if Tom Nangle knew of the difficulty with the memorial fund-raising at this point. He was still in Europe and hard at work on the battlefield memorials. On November 1, 1921 he recommended three of his War Graves staff (James Lambert, John Murphy and William Brown) for the Officer of the Order of the British Empire (O.B.E.). While Nangle himself was denied the honour of the C.M.G., he had no hesitation in pushing for three of his staff to have the O.B.E. conferred upon them. Nangle understood how difficult the work was, and how important a contribution it was to the relatives of the fallen. He did not want his staff's dedication and hard work to go unrecognized. But sadly, it would.

By early November, Governor Harris once again sent a confidential despatch to Winston Churchill in London. Harris wrote that if he understood the facts correctly, "all lists for the Order of the British Empire were closed and that it would be most unlikely that you could consider any of LCol. Father Nangle's recommendations for the O.B.E." So, it seemed that Nangle's staff would not be made members of the O.B.E. despite their tremendously difficult, agonizing work. It seemed that by now Nangle's main supporter in the cause of honours, Prime Minister Squires, had acquiesced to the Governor's way of thinking.

The Governor wrote:

> *Sir Richard Squires has now at a personal interview intimated to me that he was reluctant to revive the question of any honour for Father Nangle himself; and this gave me the*

opportunity of observing that it was not a recommendation that I could cordially support in the way it had been put.

So the question of a prestigious honour for LCol. Father Nangle was answered. History had already begun to overlook the soldier-priest.

As the year drew to a close, the War Memorial Committee again met in St. John's. On December 5, 1921, the chairman stated that "in his opinion the time had arrived when the executive must decide definitely whether it was desirable to make plans for the erection of a memorial with the funds in hand...or whether it was wiser to defer action till the times become financially brighter."

The committee had received a donation from Mr. Jas. Phelan of New York and was going to canvass the Newfoundland Society in Montreal, but the collections within Newfoundland were small "on account of the hard times." As the calendar turned on 1921, Newfoundland seemed no closer to erecting a National War Memorial. But Father Tom Nangle was about to get involved with the committee and he would make things happen.

~ CHAPTER THIRTEEN ~

FUND-RAISING

In 1922, LCol. Father Tom Nangle was still striving towards his goal of building battlefield memorials to the fallen of the Royal Newfoundland Regiment. But while he was in St. John's for Christmas, friends told him of the trouble raising money for the erection of a war memorial in the city. So, on February 3, 1922, with Prime Minister Richard Squires at his side, Nangle attended the War Memorial Committee meeting.

The chairman stated the purpose of the meeting was to hear some suggestions, and a proposition from LCol. Nangle.

Nangle informed the meeting the Imperial War Graves Commission was prepared to make an allowance of £5 sterling for every missing man of the Royal Newfoundland Regiment, Royal Naval Reserve and the Merchant Marine. The amount could total anywhere from $15,000 to $18,000. He said he felt putting this money towards the memorial was the proper thing to do under the circumstances.

At this point Father Nangle put his proposition to the executive. I am prepared, he said, "to take my coat off and work toward getting further funds for the National War Memorial...but I want an absolutely free hand as to the methods employed to raise money."

Dr. Alex Robinson supported Nangle's idea, as did Rev. Dr. Bolt. All present agreed to give Nangle a free hand to proceed with leading the development of the monument.

Before the meeting closed, Sir Richard Squires addressed the group and said "Memorial or no Memorial, the government intends to erect a Normal School, possibly on the Parade Grounds [Fort Townshend], at a cost of $100,000."

Rev Dr. Bolt opposed the idea of making the Normal School a national memorial, and Nangle agreed with him. Some of Nangle's opposition to making the Normal School a National War Memorial must have made it into the press because on February 15, 1922, Archbishop Roche wrote him the following letter:

> *The digest of your remarks which I read in the press was very brief, but from it I gathered that you expressed yourself as being strongly opposed to an educational building being erected as a War Memorial. That obviously is a question on which there is room for difference of opinion and I am sure you will admit that those who think differently are quite entitled to their own views on the matter...I think it is regrettable that the personal element should have been introduced into this matter of the National War Memorial, but for its introduction I am afraid it must be said that you yourself are primarily responsible.*

The letter suggests there was public difference of opinion over the nature and expression of the "correct" way to remember the war dead. The form and manner of a National War Memorial was something that had been argued about since the end of the war.

We speculate that veterans who had lived through the hell of war would not have been shy about expressing their opinions on the way to best remember their fallen comrades. Certainly, Father Tom Nangle was not afraid to say just what he thought about the "correct" form a National War Memorial should take.

He had been through some of the most horrific fighting of WWI and had buried his friends and comrades on the battlefields. He had to endure the unthinkable horror of revisiting those killing fields, and exhuming decaying bodies for identification and burial in organized military cemeteries. He had faced death and danger, had been shot at, bombed and wounded. He was not going to be pushed around by anyone. He would do what he thought was the right thing. If he believed in something he acted on it. That was the courage of his convictions.

Around this time, he became involved with the Great War Veteran's Association (GWVA) and Captain Gerald J. Whitty, who had been an officer with the Regiment during the war and was decorated for bravery in action. As members of the War Memorial Fund Committee, Whitty and Nangle worked closely together over the next two years. On February 18, 1922, Nangle wrote to the Archbishop, listing his return address as War Memorial Fund Office, GWVA, Water Street, St. John's.

More Fund-raising

Father Nangle formed an Action Committee to start a public fund-raising campaign for the National War Memorial. With a committee up and running, according to an article in *The Daily News*, there followed a "frenzied programme of dances, ice carnivals, sporting events and other means of raising funds." One of Nangle's schemes involved using the ski-equipped aeroplane of Major S. Cotton.

Residents of St. John's could pay a fee and go for a flight with Major Cotton in his open-cockpit, double-seater aeroplane. Fund-raising activities had already included things such as: hockey games, curling matches, concerts, lectures, an Officers' Ball, a billiard tournament, St. Patrick's Day Dance and subscribed contributions from organizations such as the Orange Lodge, Benevolent Irish Society, Clubs and Brigades, and the IWGC Grant, according to the August 1924 financial statement of the War Memorial Fund.

The Newfoundland War Memorial Company Unlimited had been established and sold shares at one dollar each, and nobody worked harder selling shares than Father Nangle.

War Memorial Committee Meeting May 8, 1922

At a War Memorial Committee on May 8, Father Nangle gave a report of his activities since taking over fund-raising in early February, announcing he had raised $48,002.34. He specified that "the brightest spot of the campaign had been the entire lack of denominational differences, all classes and creeds of the community having united to attain the objective aimed at."

Dr. Robinson then addressed the meeting and said that since Nangle had now raised the necessary funds, it was time to finally select a site for the monument. At this point, Nangle arose and made a motion:

> *WHEREAS the King's Beach is the Corner stone of the Overseas Empire, and*
> *WHEREAS the King's Beach is the site that overlooked the embarkation of so many of those for whom the monument will stand and also overlooked the returned of the broken and the maimed and,*
> *WHEREAS it is the only site of easy access in the city and may be seen by all who enter or leave our harbor, and*
> *WHEREAS it is the only site approved by the general public, BE IT RESOLVED that this executive of the National War Memorial Committee decide that the National War Memorial be erected on the King's Beach.*

His motion was seconded by A.W. Mews (and Major J.W. March) and was carried unanimously.

Nangle then addressed the meeting and gave his idea for the form of the memorial. Inspired by Colonel John MacRae's moving poem In Flanders Fields, he suggested having the monument as "a leading light," a figure holding up the torch that MacRae referred to in his poem.

Father Nangle had certainly moved the reality of a war memorial along. In a short time he had got into fund-raising, and he was leading the site selection as well as making suggestions about that shape and form of the monument.

Another meeting of the executive of the War Memorial Committee was held on June 17, 1922. Nangle was still in St. John's and attended this meeting which included: Capt Gerald Whitty, A.W. Mews, City Councillor Outerbridge, Lady Crosbie, Mrs. Eric Ayre, and Miss Mary Keegan.

Mr. D.M. Baird moved that another committee be struck to finalize the work on the memorial, and suggested it consist of Nangle, Whitty and at least one other. This was seconded by J.G. Higgins and carried unanimously. A general discussion followed which favored turning the finished monument over to the government in trust.

By late August, Father Nangle had returned to Europe, accompanied by Prime Minister Squires. On Sunday, August 27, 1922, Squires unveiled a memorial tablet in the Cathedral in Amiens, France. Nangle and other Newfoundland veterans attended.

In an article in the December 1922 issue of *The Veteran* magazine, Nangle wrote about the unveiling, saying that in towns like Amiens, Cambrai, Arras, and Ypres, tablets would be erected in cathedrals in memory of the Royal Newfoundland Regiment. The Colours of the Regiment would accompany the memorial tablet.

The tablet was made from lunel marble and was designed by M. Moreau, Architect-in-Chief of the Ministry of Fine Arts. The inscription was suggested by Mr. Rudyard Kipling.

The tablet erected by Newfoundland stood alongside memorial plaques to the soldiers of Canada, Australia, South Africa and the United States of America. These were the nations that had come to free France from the tyranny of German occupation.

At the start of the ceremony the tablet was draped with the tricolor and the Union Jack. Prime Minister Squires opened the proceedings and apologized for his lack of proficiency in the French language. Squires stated: "On behalf of the people of Newfoundland, I consequently ask you to accept for your cathedral this war memorial and flag of our island."

M. Dormond accepted the memorial tablet and flag on behalf of the French people. He said: "I assure you of our undying gratefulness to the soldiers from Newfoundland who fell in France." At the conclusion of his remarks, Dormond unveiled the plaque by removing the tricolor and Union Jack accompanied by a bugler playing the Last Post. Monsignor Mantel then dedicated and blessed the tablet.

Prime Minister Squires placed a wreath from the people of Newfoundland, while Staff-Sgt. Majors Murphy and Hutchings placed another of red and white roses - the colors of the Regiment - on behalf of the Great War Veteran's Association.

The following week, Squires visited Etaples Cemetery along with Padre Nangle and placed another wreath on the Cross of

Sacrifice in remembrance of the other Newfoundlanders killed in France and Belgium. Squires also laid an individual wreath on the grave of each Newfoundlander buried in Etaples.

On September 7, 1922, Nangle was in London, England, and wrote to R.G. Rendell concerning the St. John's War Memorial. He said he had given Gotto first chance of presenting a design. He also said he could get granite from Italy cheaper than from Newfoundland, provided that some St. John s merchant would donate passage on a ship. Nangle was clearly using every means possible to get the National War Memorial built. He literally scrounged, begged and borrowed as necessary.

Nangle told Rendell he was in a peculiar position during the fund-raising campaign, "I didn't care if I offended people or not," he said. When Nangle got involved with the War Memorial Committee he made things happen. He had a goal in sight to honour the fallen of the Regiment and he went straight for it.

On September 19, 1922, after Squires returned to Newfoundland, Father Nangle attended the regular monthly meeting of the Imperial War Graves Commission. He was still engrossed in the work of commemorating the war dead of the Royal Newfoundland Regiment.

On October 11, Nangle was in London and wrote R.G. Rendell again. He said things in Europe were moving slowly but satisfactorily with Major Howe Greene and Captain Basil Gotto working on models of the National War Memorial. Nangle said the first caribou memorial was in place, adding, "If we are as successful with our St. John's memorial as we are with our memorials in France, I do not think there will be any cause for complaint."

Rudolph Cochius, Landscape Architect

By late October 1922, Father Tom Nangle had met landscape architect Rudolph Cochius. Born in Arnhem, Holland, Cochius was known to Newfoundlanders as the man who designed and built Bowring Park in St. John's for Sir Edgar Bowring as part of the 100th anniversary celebrations of Bowring Brothers Limited. He worked on the park from 1912 - 1917.

In an October 31, 1922 letter to Mrs. Janet Ayre, Hon. Secretary of the Beaumont Hamel Collection Committee, Nangle advised that he had taken Cochius over the ground in France and they had talked things over and he could tell her what they would like. By October 1923, the Beaumont Hamel Collection Committee had raised $8,815 which was used to help pay for the development of the memorial park. Citizen fund-raising was to play a big part in both the Memorial Park in Beaumont Hamel, and the National War Memorial in St. John's. Father Tom Nangle figured prominently in both funding drives.

On November 4, 1922, Cochius cabled a three page outline of his plan for the Beaumont Hamel Memorial Park to Nangle.

~ Chapter Fourteen ~
COCHIUS' VISION

Rudolph Cochius was a visionary and a very talented man. He could take a piece of ground and turn it into a masterpiece. That was what he did in St. John's where he turned Rae Island Farm on the outskirts of St. John's into a lovely nature park (Bowring Park). He would accomplish the same thing with Beaumont Hamel Memorial Park. Hugh Nangle remembers his father praising Cochius for creating such a wonderful park at Beaumont Hamel.

In his proposal, Cochius congratulated Nangle on selecting Beaumont Hamel as the site for a memorial park. He said what better way to commemorate the battle fought there than "by partly preserving this field, where so many Newfoundlanders have died, in its original state, with its trenches, its no man's land and its graves."

Cochius emphasized that the historic value of the place, coupled with its natural attractions, meant that development work should be carried out in such a way that it would harmonize with the surroundings.

One of the most important things to be considered...is to provide a suitable entrance...which should be dignified without being elaborate and at the same time serve as an index to the general character of the park itself. With such an entrance one realizes at once he is passing into a place of importance...This is also one of the places where spruces (if possible Newfoundland white-spruce) should be thickly planted, on both sides of the entrance and along the fence.

Cochius' plan discussed issues like creating a driveway, pathways and a rain shelter. He estimated the entire cost at between $25,000 and $30,000, not including the monument or fence. He said he would spend about $20,000 in the first year of construction, and the remaining $5,000 - $10,000 in the following two years.

The landscape architect proposed two methods of payment for his services. The first involved him moving to France and living near the site where he could directly supervise the building. For this option, he asked for $120 dollars a month, with moving expenses paid and a guarantee of two years work.

As an alternative, he said he could remain in Arnhem and visit the site as much as required. This would cost $30 per week with travel costs. Cochius suggested the first alternative would be best for both parties.

He ended his proposal by making some brief comments about the proposed caribou memorials for Masnieres and Gueudecourt.

Nangle was not only corresponding with Cochius regarding the creation of Beaumont Hamel Memorial Park, he was continuing his work with the war graves. On November 9, 1922, he wrote to Prime Minister Squires in connection with the erection of permanent markers on the graves of the fallen. He said the plan was to remove the temporary wooden crosses and erect stone crosses.

This plan included sending the wooden crosses home to the next of kin in Newfoundland. Some people felt it was more suitable to send home the nameplate, not the entire wooden cross.

In a November 9, 1922 letter to Prime Minister Squires, Nangle said the "first shipment of crosses was sent to Newfoundland on August 14, 1922...sixteen crosses."

He penned a separate two-page letter to Squires regarding the properties now held by Newfoundland in France and Belgium. He wrote:

> *In accordance with the policy adopted by Newfoundland in 1919, I have secured various sites in France and Belgium for the erection of Newfoundland War Memorials. With the exception of Beaumont Hamel these properties are of small extent and the horticultural treatment can be easily attended to but at Beaumont Hamel...where it was the intention of the Government to build a proper 'Memorial Park'...it is necessary that a trained, experienced and expert landscape architect should be retained for the purpose of planning and supervising the work. This man I have obtained in the person of Mr. R.H.K.Cochius, who owing to his vast experience in Newfoundland, could not be improved upon as the man for this work....the sum he recommends to be spent is between 25 and 30 thousand dollars. This amount would be spread over a period of two years and is inclusive of his own services at a guaranteed salary of $120 per month for that period....I understand some $7,000 has already been collected for the beautifying of Beaumont Hamel and is in the possession of the Beaumont Hamel Collection Committee. This leaves a minimum balance of say $18,000 for the construction of the Park ....I hope you will see your way clear to guide me as to the line of action that the Government intends to pursue in the matter of this Memorial Park at Beaumont Hamel.*

This letter is important because it shows that Nangle had contracted Cochius, and set in motion development of the almost 84 acres of Beaumont Hamel Memorial Park. The letter also discussed the fund-raising that had gone on for the establishment of the park and noted $7,000 had been collected by the Beaumont Hamel Collection Committee. While Nangle had been working on the old battlefront, the citizens of Newfoundland and no doubt veterans had been working hard to support the idea of a memorial to the sacrifice at Beaumont Hamel.

By December, Squires had granted Nangle permission to move ahead with Cochius' plan. On December 30, 1922, Cochius had a scale drawing of the Beaumont Hamel Park finalized. But it would be two years and some months before Father Tom Nangle would help unveil Gotto s mighty stag amidst Cochius' manicured landscape.

During the time he spent working on the Beaumont Hamel Park, Cochius and his wife unveiled an addition to their family, Rudolph Jr. As he toiled hard in building a fitting memorial for the dead soldiers of Newfoundland at Beaumont Hamel, Cochius had no idea that in a few short years his namesake would die helping to liberate France from German occupation. Twenty-year-old Rudolph Cochius Jr. was part of the Cameron Highlanders of the Canadian Army in World War II and made the supreme sacrifice on Juno Beach on June 7, 1944. He is buried in Normandy.

~ CHAPTER FIFTEEN ~

BUILDING A NATIONAL MEMORIAL

On February 1, 1923, Nangle was in London, and wrote R.G. Rendell in St. John's regarding work on the monument for the city.

LCol. Robert Rendell had commanded the Church Lads Brigade from 1904 to 1918 and ably assisted in recruiting for the Regiment in 1914.

On June 9, 1921, following a motion by Mr. P.E. Outerbridge, he was acclaimed as chairman of the new National War Memorial Committee. He and his committee worked tirelessly for years in the quest to establish a fitting memorial for the service personnel who fought and died in WW1. The committee also strongly supported Nangle's efforts to make this dream a reality. In his letter, Nangle informed Rendell he was forwarding photographs of the model for the monument and that four of the five bronze figures were in the hands of the founders.

In a related correspondence to Rendell dated October 11, 1922, Nangle said, "We have our first caribou in place, and it looks very very fine. I wish Sir Edgar Bowring had presented one of the these to Bowring Park."

Nangle's wish later came true as Sir Edgar's cousin, Major William Howe Green, donated a full sized caribou, a replica of the ones in Europe, to Bowring Park. The unveiling took place July 1, 1928, Newfoundland's Memorial Day.

On March 5, 1923, Outerbridge wrote Rendell, saying "my ideas regarding the designs sent out by Nangle are that I don't like any of them. In fact now I favor the cross idea..."

It seems the road to constructing the National War Memorial was still full of pitfalls, mine fields, and hurdles for Father Tom Nangle.

Later that same month, Nangle made yet another Atlantic crossing and returned to St. John's. *The Veteran* magazine of April 1923 reported "the many friends of Padre Nangle, of whom they are legion, were delighted to welcome him back again on his arrival from England."

Nangle was described as being in good health and showed no "signs of diminishing enthusiasm regarding the National War Memorial and Newfoundland Battle Memorials." It was said he'd come to St. John's in connection with the National War Memorial.

During his time in the city, he attended an "At Home" sponsored by the Great War Veteran's Association. The guest list included Governor and Lady Allardyce, Sir Richard Squires, Mayor Tasker Cook and the former Minister of Militia, the Hon. J.R. Bennett.

April's issue of *The Veteran* magazine stated, "To LCol. T. Nangle, the GWVA owe a debt of gratitude...the interest shown by this Officer in affairs pertaining to the welfare of the GWVA is second to none, and we tender him our sincere and grateful thanks."

The Great War Veterans Association (GWVA) was an organization founded after WW1 to address the needs of returning Newfoundland veterans. The GWVA established branches throughout Newfoundland.

Also in April, *The Veteran* magazine reported that:

> *Plans and models for the National War Memorial are now on exhibition at the Board of Trade Building, St. John's. It is hoped that co-incident with the arrival of LCol. T. Nangle (C.F.) from England, one of the models submitted will be accepted, and specifications and costs put in order...*

Nangle had been untiring in his efforts to push forward the scheme with as little delay as possible. On July 17th, Nangle, wearing his Roman collar, chaired a dinner of Newfoundland's Great War Veterans in London, in "honour of the delegates of the British Empire Service League."

That same month, *The Veteran* magazine reported that completion of the National War Memorial in St. John's had advanced beyond the visionary stage. The Finalization Committee had met with and the GWVA Dominion Command to survey three plaster models of various designs that had arrived form England. Model number three was chosen and Nangle was empowered to put the construction orders in place at once.

The memorial was planned for King's Beach in St. John's, and it was hoped to hold the unveiling on July 1, 1924. *The Veteran* magazine reported:

> *LCol. Nangle is untiring in his efforts to arrange a ceremony which will be worthy of the occasion, and with this end in view it is proposed to invite our Allies to be represented by Naval detachments.*

It was also intended to ask the King to consent to unveil the memorial. Nangle hoped to return to St. John's in the early spring of 1924 to supervise the final construction and organize the unveiling ceremonies. "*The erection of Newfoundland's National War Memorial will be a tribute from a proud and grateful kinsfolk to the Honored Dead it perpetuates.*"

Also in July 1923, Nangle's strong supporter, Prime Minister Richard Squires was forced to resign from office because of accusations that his government was involved with inappropriate use of public funds. As a result, William R. Warren was sworn in as Prime Minister and he established a public enquiry under British lawyer T. Hollis Walker to examine the claims against the Squires' Government.

The political shake up at home did not seem to affect Nangle's work. He returned to Europe to continue his efforts with War Graves Registration and Enquiries, but Newfoundland was never far from his mind.

In the October 1923 issue of *The Veteran* magazine, he wrote a letter to the editor in which he proposed leading a four-week pilgrimage to the battlefields of France and Belgium in September 1924:

> *I have covered the route during the past summer with representatives of the leading European travel agencies and have received from them estimates on which they are prepared to undertake a contract. I have also interviewed the leading shipping companies and am convinced I can carry out my program for the sum advertised this Spring, viz. $300.00, provided I can secure sufficient pilgrims.*

Nangle explained that the $300 would cover first class steamer to France, and then train travel within France. He emphasized he would endeavour to give every relative who had a soldier with a known grave an opportunity of visiting that grave. He aimed to get 500 pilgrims, and asked people to write to him in care of the GWVA and express their intentions to go.

Captain Gerald Whitty, an executive member of the GWVA, wrote a lengthy article in the October issue of *The Veteran* describing his visit to battlefields in France and Belgium with

Nangle: *"I was very much impressed by the splendid efforts put forward by the Newfoundland Government through its representative, Colonel Nangle, to perpetuate the glorious memory of our men who died during the war."*

He said Nangle was of the opinion that the National War Memorial should be completed for the planned unveiling of July 1, 1924.

Nangle traveled tirelessly throughout Newfoundland and made an appeal for financial help. He went to many tiny, isolated outports to visit families who had lost loved ones in the war.

On October 22, 1923, the first rock cliff at King's Beach was blasted to make way for the National War Memorial. According to *The Veteran* magazine, Governor Allardyce lit the fuse in front of thousands of people. The "contract for the preliminary concreting of the plateau was awarded to Messrs. Churchill and Pearce, both of whom are ex-servicemen."

On November 25, Nangle left St. John's for Boston where he had been invited by the Boston-Newfoundland Mutual Benefit Association. He gave a lecture on the Royal Newfoundland Regiment at the Municipal Building on Shawmut Avenue in Boston. He also talked about the building of the National War Memorial in St. John's.

As 1923 drew to a close, Nangle was inching closer towards realizing his goal of a series of battlefield memorials in Europe and a National War Memorial in St. John's. The combination of his drive and persistence, coupled with the talent of others such as landscape architect Rudolph Cochius, sculptor Basil Gotto, Capt. Gerald Whitty of the GWVA, and the vision of women like Lady Crosbie, Mrs. Eric Ayre, and Mrs. Keegan, and others on the National War Memorial Committee, was paying dividends.

~ CHAPTER SIXTEEN ~

UNVEILING

In 1924, much of Nangle's work was beginning to bear fruit. In a letter dated February 13, 1924, Gerald Whitty advised R. G. Rendell he had heard from Nangle and that everything was in first class condition.

Nangle was coming to Newfoundland shortly and intending to bring some of the national memorial statuary with him. Three of the five figures (the sailor, forester and merchant marine) were completely finished and the female figure representing Newfoundland was to be finished that week. Whitty said the plaster cast of the last figure (the soldier) was handed to the bronze foundry on January 26th.

"I anticipate that Colonel Nangle will be coming on the return trip of the Digby which is en route to Liverpool at present," he concluded.

In March of that year, Nangle was selected as the new president of the GWVA. As if he didn't have enough to do, he now had another hat to wear. He seemed to prove the old saying "if you want something done, ask a busy person to do it."

On March 21, T. Hollis Walker released his report on the alleged wrongdoings of the Squires' Administration resulting in charges being pressed against the Prime Minister. By mid-April, Nangle and ex-servicemen had become active in the campaign against government corruption. Rumours of an ex-servicemen's political party swirled through the country. Father Nangle addressed a crowded gathering of the GWVA in the Star Theatre in St. John's. The Prime Minister, Hon. W.R. Warren, was in attendance. *The Daily News* ran the headline "Padre Nangle Delivers Forceful and Inspiring Address."

Nangle said the purpose of his address was to remind veterans of their duty to themselves, their comrades, country and God. In his lengthy address, he touched on many issues including the fact some ex-servicemen had fallen into heavy drinking and needed assistance. He asked those present if they could help billet out-harbour veterans who would be in St. John's for Field Marshal Haig's visit and unveiling of the National War Monument in July. He said:

> *The Great War Veterans Association is a non-sectarian body. We knew no creed in France. I challenge anyone who served overseas whether I ever asked what his religion was. I have treated you as man to man....there was no such thing as sectarianism in France, and as long as I am honored with the position of the executive head of the GWVA there will be no sectarianism...Besides being non-sectarian, our association is non-political...if the Walker Report has done nothing else it has awakened public morality in Newfoundland....The time has come in Newfoundland for all civil service positions to be filled by competitive examination...we demand that disabled ex-servicemen be given first priority...We demand that every ex-service man in this country be given the right to work for his living without having to go abroad....It has been rumoured we are forming an ex-serviceman's party, but we do not at present intend to form any such party although we have the machinery to put in motion to cleanse our politics from sectarianism and corrupt practices....*

Tom Nangle was a forceful public speaker. He was used to preaching from the pulpit, plus he had the self-assuredness of an athlete coupled with the confidence of a man who had survived combat. He knew how to deliver a message in a moving, thought-provoking manner.

Following Nangle's speech, Prime Minister Warren promised the government would pay travel costs for all ex-servicemen coming to St. John's for Haig's visit and the unveiling of the National War Memorial.

Cochius

While the rumour mill about former Prime Minister Squire and a party of ex-servicemen was swirling, landscape architect Rudolph Cochius wrote an article titled "Marking the Trail of the Caribou," which appeared in the April issue of *The Veteran* magazine:

> *It is now sixteen months since Colonel Nangle came to see me in Holland and invited me to inspect with him the sites for the Newfoundland War Memorials in France and Belgium...to perpetuate forever the Trail of the Caribou.*

Cochius went on to say that though Newfoundland was a tiny Dominion in the vast British Empire, its war memorials would be as good as that of any other Dominion. He wrote:

> *The Canadians, the South Africans, the Australians, the New Zealanders are all doing great things in commemorating their Dead and their deeds and are spending millions in doing so. We will not, however, stand one foot behind any of them and though their millions will only be thousands in this case, Beaumont Hamel Park will not stand behind Vimy-Ridge Park or Delville-Wood (called the Devil's Wood by the South Africans)...it will be the impressiveness of the whole place that will make the Newfoundland Park at Beaumont Hamel a place of pilgrimage...*

Cochius was certain his design, his creation, and his adaptation of Nangle's idea for the Beaumont Hamel Memorial would stand the test of time.

To support his claim, he quoted the Australian Prime Minister, Mr. Bruce, who had fought on the Western Front as a Captain in the 29th Division. Bruce visited Beaumont Hamel and was most impressed with the development proceeding there. He said of all that he had seen, the Newfoundland Park at Beaumont Hamel was the most impressive and artistic memorial on the whole of the battle line.

Cochius explained in some detail that Father Nangle had decided it was important to preserve, as much as possible, the battlefield, no man's land, trenches and dugouts of Beaumont Hamel as "a perpetual reminder for future generations - as a sacred ground."

In the following year, the Memorial Park at Beaumont Hamel was officially unveiled by Field Marshal Haig, who was accompanied by his Aide-de-Camp, LCol. Father Tom Nangle. But that momentous occasion would have to wait. There was another monument to christen; namely the National War Memorial in St. John's.

Earl Haig Arrives in Newfoundland

On Sunday June 29, 1924 at 10 a.m. the steamship Caronia docked at King's Wharf in St. John's harbour. On board were Field Marshal Douglas Haig and Lady Haig. Haig had been the Commander-in-Chief of the British Expeditionary Force from December 10, 1915 until the final, successful Allied advance in 1918.

During his week long visit to Newfoundland, LCol. Father Tom Nangle served as Aide-de-Camp to Haig. He would continue to serve in that position into the following year, when the Beaumont Hamel Memorial Park was unveiled and a tour of Canada conducted.

The Haigs were met by a "Guard of Honour, including returned soldiers, a large number of civic and government officials, and other citizens," according to The Newfoundland Quarterly. After formal greetings, presentation of floral bouquets and the like, the Haigs went to Government House with Governor and Lady Allardyce. For the next week, there was a busy schedule of social events. But the crowning jewel of the visit was the unveiling of the National War Memorial on Tuesday July 1, 1924.

The Unveiling of the National War Memorial

The unveiling happened eight years to the day after the Battle of Beaumont Hamel July 1, 1916. At 10 a.m. on the morning of July 1, 1924 a huge parade of an estimated 2,500 soldiers, sailors, veterans, mounted Constabulary, Cadets, Girl Guides and Boy Scouts marched past the Court House on Water Street in St. John's. Haig took the salute from a reviewing stand. The weather was reported by *The Daily News* to be "gloriously fine...with the sun shining in all its glory."

> *At the appointed hour, His Excellency the Governor and Field Marshal Haig arrived (at the veiled War Memorial) and were received with presented arms by a guard of honor.*

The new Prime Minister, Walter S. Monroe, who had taken over after the 1924 election, was present to welcome Haig, as was the Mayor of St. John's, Tasker Cook.

Chairman R.G. Rendell addressed the crowd and dignitaries on behalf of the War Memorial Committee. Governor William L. Allardyce accepted the monument on behalf of the people of

Newfoundland. Allardyce was a career military officer who served as governor from 1922 - 1928. In his acceptance speech he stated:

> *I formally accept, on behalf of the people of Newfoundland and its Dependencies, this National War Memorial. Close to this historic and commanding spot Sir Humphrey Gilbert landed in August 1583 and in taking possession in the name of his sovereign, Queen Elizabeth, of this New Found Land thereby founded our Overseas Empire. Every Newfoundlander knows what this Memorial represents, and we are profoundly grateful that it is to be unveiled today by one who led our armies to victory...*

Following the Governor's remarks there were prayers by various church leaders including Rev. Broughton, president of the Methodist Conference and The Rt. Rev. J. March, Bishop of Harbour Grace. The unveiling of the memorial was a non-denominational affair.

After the prayers, a firing party shot three volleys, then a bugler played the "Last Post" which was followed by two minutes of silence. Field Marshal Haig then addressed the huge crowd and began his remarks by saying:

> *Your Excellency, Colonel Nangle, Ladies and Gentlemen: It is an honour which I deeply appreciate to be given this opportunity to associate myself with the tribute which Newfoundland pays to her gallant dead...I am here not only as your old leader in the field, but as the representative...of those armies from great Britain and the other Dominions who fought with you the Empire's battles and today are proud to join with you in honoring the brave sons of Newfoundland who died...*

Haig continued speaking for some time. He thanked the parents present and expressed his sympathy to the families who had lost sons, brothers, fathers in the conflict. He praised the fighting record of the Royal Newfoundland Regiment and made special mention of the Regiment's defense of Masnieres during late November 1917. He concluded, "In memory of our gallant comrades, who gave their lives for King and Country, I unveil this monument."

That evening, Haig addressed a gathering of ex-servicemen at the Church Lads Brigade Armoury. Nangle accompanied Haig to the speaking platform in the front of the hall and opened the meeting by welcoming the former Commander-in-Chief.

He said the veterans felt proud of the honour paid them by the visit of the distinguished soldier who had come to unveil a memorial to their gallant comrades. He went on to implore the ex-servicemen to be as good citizens as they had been soldiers. Finally, on behalf of the GWVA, he presented Haig with a silver caribou mounted on a pedestal - a replica of the caribou memorials to be found in Europe.

On July 3, a public reception was held at Bannerman Park to give as many citizens as possible a chance to greet Haig. Once again, Nangle, along with GWVA executive member Captain Whitty, met Haig at the park and escorted him to the speaking platform, along with Capt. V.S. Bennett.

That evening the Sergeant's Mess of the Royal Newfoundland Regiment sponsored a dinner in Haig's honor. The following day, a garden party was held at Government House.

A regatta was also held during "Haig Week" as the visit came to be known. Nangle attended the regatta in his Roman collar and black suit.

Later in the week, Haig spent some time angling on the Salmonier River. Accompanied by Nangle, he also made time to lay wreaths on veterans' graves at Belvedere, Mount Carmel, General Protestant and Church of England cemeteries.

On Tuesday July 8, the Haig visit came to an end. They boarded the steamship *Caronia* for the voyage back to England. The Newfoundland Quarterly reported that during his week in Newfoundland Haig had talked about citizenship and not militarism.

Forty years after the National War Memorial was unveiled in St. John's, Tom Nangle told his son Hugh about Field Marshal Haig:

> *Dad talked about Haig as being a pretty dour Scotsman. But he was a very religious man who really felt strongly about his troops and that there were so many lives sacrificed." When it came to being an Aide-de-Camp for Haig, his father said it was important to always be well prepared. "Dad said that you had to be meticulously prepared for Haig. He expected an enormous amount from his staff. One had to be clean-shaven, impeccably dressed and well-mannered at all times.*

Hugh believes his father got on so well with Haig because he himself was a man who paid close attention to details:

> *Dad worked from the premise that if you took care of the small things, the big things would fall into place because one had prepared meticulously. Haig liked that sort of preparedness.*

Nangle remained close to Haig. They officially opened the memorial park at Beaumont Hamel in 1925. Even after Lord Haig's death in 1928, Lady Haig stayed in contact with Tom Nangle.

On July 29, 1924 the Dominion Headquarters of the GWVA sent its members a letter soliciting "contributions from 25 cents up" for the purpose of making a presentation to LCol..Nangle on behalf of ex-servicemen and next-of-kin. The letter said the presentation would be made in the coming weeks in St. John's and was signed by Gerald Whitty, Dominion Secretary of the GWVA. But while the GWVA wanted to make a presentation to Nangle for all his hard work, his labour was not yet complete.

On September 8, 1924, he left St. John's to return to France. He parted company with his friend and comrade Captain Whitty. It was little the men knew this would be their final parting. On September 15, while attending a dinner with Royal Naval visitors in Donovans [just outside St. John's], Whitty was killed by a speeding automobile. Whitty had lived through the horrors of battle on the Western Front and Gallipoli. He was killed by a negligent driver who was convicted of manslaughter. Nangle was saddened and shocked to learn of the sudden passing of his dear friend, a man who had worked hard on the development of the National War Memorial. At Whitty's grave side, Nangle observed sadly that veterans had lost their best friend and advocate.

But as he had during the war, Tom Nangle "soldiered on," and on September 28, 1924 he was at the unveiling of the 51st Highland Division Memorial in Beaumont Hamel Newfoundland Memorial Park. French Field Marshal Foch unveiled this monument.

The Veteran magazine reported, "The Padre is continuing his work caring for Newfoundland's war graves and Memorials on the other side, and from recent reports he is going full steam ahead in this connection."

~ Chapter Seventeen ~
TRAIL OF THE CARIBOU COMPLETED

In 1925, Nangle completed his work in marking the "Trail of the Caribou." But he continued to strive to do more to commemorate the dead of the Royal Newfoundland Regiment.

On February 14, 1925, he wrote to Captain Stair Gillon regarding a history of the 29th Division that Gillon was writing. During the war, it was constantly remarked that the 29th Division possessed a unity or divisional spirit unequaled by any other formation. The Newfoundland Regiment proudly served as a part of this great fighting unit.

Nangle asked Gillon if he was interested in writing the history of the Royal Newfoundland Regiment. His letter stated:

> *At the end of the War the then Colonial Secretary of Newfoundland gave the writing of the History of the Royal Newfoundland Regiment to F.A.MacKenzie but as this gentleman was distasteful to the ex-servicemen no one would put any records at his disposal. As a result nothing has so far been done. Being the President of the Ex-Service Men's Organization in Newfoundland, I should like to know what the cost would be of writing this proposed Regimental History and whether, or not you would be prepared to take on the proposition.*

Nangle, though nearing the end of his work with graves registration and battlefield monument creation, was labouring to ensure that the sacrifice of the Royal Newfoundland Regiment was enshrined in words. He continued to be a man with many irons in the fire.

We know today that the story of the Royal Newfoundland Regiment was told by Richard Cramm, and later by Col. G.W.L. Nicholson, whose book entitled *"The Fighting Newfoundander"* is often referred to as the bible on the Regiment's First World War history.

But at that time, Nangle was striving to get the Regiment's story recorded for future generations. Again, we see his interest in and commitment to enshrining history.

But Tom Nangle was not all work and no play. In the winter of 1925 he was part of an English hockey team, The London Lions, which was entered in an international hockey tournament in Switzerland. No doubt the many games of hockey he had played in his youth with St. Bon's College had prepared him for this challenge.

Beaumont Hamel Unveiled

On June 7, 1925, under beautiful weather conditions, the caribou memorial at Beaumont Hamel was officially dedicated and unveiled by Field Marshal Haig accompanied by LCol. Nangle. A large crowd was present for the unveiling ceremony, composed of numerous religious, civic and military dignitaries: Marshal Fayolle, Chief of French general staff; J.R. Bennett; LCol. A.E. Bernard and wife; Lt. General Sir Almer and Lady Hunter-Weston; Lt. General Sir Beauvoir de Lisle; Major W.H. and Mrs. Parsons; Major General D.E. Cayley; LCol. A.L. Hadow; Captain and Mrs. Basil Gotto; Mr. and Mrs. Rudolf Cochius, and many others, relatives and friends of the Regiment. Each of the units of the renowned 29th Division sent representatives for the honour guard.

The years of hard work, negotiations, fund-raising and worry had come to an end. Finally, the hallowed ground at Beaumont Hamel was ready to serve as a shrine to the sacrifice of the North Atlantic Dominion.

Nangle later said that the park dedication could not have been held on July 1 because Haig had to be in Canada for meetings with veterans. As Haig's Aide-de-Camp, Nangle had to leave for Canada a week earlier for planning preparations.

The Daily News of June 9, 1925 reported on the official opening. The Hon. J.R. Bennett represented the government of Newfoundland and he opened the proceedings with an address. This was followed by a speech from Field Marshal Haig:

> *We are here to unveil a Memorial which will remind generations still unborn of the Newfoundland men, and of the unity and strength of the mighty Empire which is our pride and inheritance...These slopes where fell so many of your best and bravest are sacred to their memory. Here your comrades died in the hope of that victory they would never see; today that victory achieved, you set up in the place where they died a Monument to their faith and courage. This spot will become a place of pilgrimage which, generation after generation, will draw Newfoundlanders to France. The Battalion added a glorious and never to be forgotten chapter to the honorable history of England's Oldest Colony.*

Following Haig's address, the Last Post was sounded by buglers of the Royal Scots Regiment and the memorial was dedicated by the Vicar General of Amiens. Marshal La Fayolle of the French Army also delivered a "stirring address." After the speeches, many wreaths were laid on the monument. Two of Rudolph Cochius' daughters laid a wreath on behalf of the children of Newfoundland.

In July, Haig and Nangle toured Canada. A newspaper clipping shows a picture of both of them and the caption says that Haig is "with his A.D.C. Col. Nangle, who arranged his present tour and accompanies him." Part of this tour involved Haig and Nangle helping to establish the Royal Canadian Legion.

The year 1925 was memorable because Memorial University College and the adjacent Normal School opened on the parade grounds near Fort Townshend in St. John's. Englishman John Lewis Paton was the college's first president. Despite the controversy over the shape and form of a war memorial, Newfoundland now had both a National War Monument and a Memorial College.

1926

In May 1926, *The Veteran* magazine carried a story written by Nangle about the creation of Beaumont- Hamel Park. He makes it clear he had a significant amount of political help in developing the park:

> *I wish to go on record here that to Sir Richard Squires and Sir William Coaker Newfoundland owes the fact that her sons are commemorated in a fashion worthy of Newfoundland. On every occasion these two gentlemen when approached gave me unlimited authority to do what I thought was right. Mr. Warren and Mr. Monroe have also given me help and support in completing the work at hand.*

W. S. Monroe was Prime Minister from 1924-28 while William R. Warren was the Prime Minister who replaced Squires during the scandal of 1923. Nangle made a point of praising his old ally Squires who, along with Coaker, had done much to commemorate Newfoundland's glorious fallen.

Nangle explained that the bronze caribous actually cost £750 each, not £1000. He had completed blazing the "Trail of the Caribou" through Europe and "Five Monarchs of the Topsails" marked important battlegrounds where Newfoundlanders had bravely fought and died.

One can only imagine the immense void that faced the soldier-priest. What had been his life's work, his reason for being, what had occupied his every waking moment for the past eight years was now completed.

His work was finished and he was about to make a major career move. Sometime around 1926 an important event occurred in his life. He decided to leave the priesthood and move to Rhodesia, South Africa. In the late 1920's it was practically unheard of for a man to leave the priesthood. Unfortunately, no documents pertaining to his decision to leave the priesthood, or the Roman Catholic church's response to his resignation, could be located.

~ Chapter Eighteen ~
LEAVING THE PRIESTHOOD

One might wonder how Tom Nangle selected Rhodesia as a place to settle. According to Hugh, his father was thinking about moving to Australia but was advised that the Roman Catholic church was very strong there and it might be an uncomfortable place for a former priest to live. He may have seen Rhodesia as a quiet place, free from the prying eyes of the judgmental world.

Another reason Nangle went to Rhodesia may have been its warm, dry climate. Hugh says his father got trench foot during the war and cold, damp weather made it act up and "almost crippled him."

Still another factor may have influenced his decision to go to Rhodesia. At the third Biennial Conference of the British Empire Service League (BESL), the South African delegate, Sir Abe Bailey, presented the League with a land grant of 10,000 acres. Bailey had helped win this territory for the Empire and "was now endeavoring to have it peopled with men of the right type."

Tom Nangle attended the BESL conference, which was opened by his old friend Earl Haig. The availability of free agricultural land, the warm climate, and its remoteness were likely all factors which influenced Nangle to choose Rhodesia as a place to settle.

Perhaps more pressure was placed on him when his comrade and friend, Earl Haig, died on January 28, 1928. This was the latest in a string of people close to him who had died when he was making major life decisions.

Archbishop Howley, who had ordained Nangle, died in October 1914 just as the young priest was striving to get to the Front. Then in 1916, his mother died while he was in France. His close friend and comrade, Gerald Whitty, was killed tragically by an automobile after Nangle returned to Europe following the unveiling of the National War Memorial in 1924. During the war he lost many comrades, friends, school chums and sports teammates. It was a seeming pattern that people close to him were ripped out of his life. At age forty, with the "Trail of the Caribou" clearly marked, it is understandable that Tom Nangle looked for someone to share his life.

So, it is not surprising that on October 12, 1929, the former priest wed Thelma Watkinson, a native Rhodesian who was 20 years his junior.

The couple settled in the village of Que-Que (pronounced KwekKwek) and raised a family of four children. Timothy Haig Nangle was born in 1930 and named after Earl Haig, Hugh was born in 1935, Rory in 1940 and Mavourneen in 1942.

Lady Haig was godmother to Timothy Haig Nangle. In 1930, she went out to Rhodesia for his christening and to visit the Nangle family. It was a grueling excursion. After a long boat trip to Cape Town, South Africa, Hugh said, she had to spend five days in a train to get to Hunter's Road, Rhodesia:

> *Lady Haig was apparently very fond of my father. I remember my mother saying that she treated Dad like a member of her family. Mother used to joke that it was a bit of an inspection tour by Lady Haig to view LCol. Nangle's new bride and son.*

Mother said Lady Haig said that Dad was the best Aide-de-Camp her husband ever had.

His father hardly ever talked about the priesthood and Hugh said his mother only talked about the matter once when he was fifteen, and that was during an election campaign when some derogatory comments had been made about his father by a neighbour.

When asked why he thinks his father left the priesthood, Hugh says it's because he lost his faith after the war. "What he saw visited on individuals and families was horrendous and he lost his faith as a direct result. Also, I think the Roman Catholic church tried to rein him in and he refused to accept this."

Tom Nangle made a living on Hunter's Road in Que-Que principally by farming. But in 1932 he defeated W.M. Leggate and was elected to the Rhodesian Legislature as a member of the Reform Party, a party he helped to found. It seems he had not lost his desire to accomplish things. He was defeated in the next election in Salisbury District by Prime Minister Godfrey Huggins. He later ran unsuccessfully in several other elections as a Labour candidate. But Tom Nangle enjoyed greater success in municipal politics and was Deputy Mayor of Que-Que for some time.

While Nangle was living in Rhodesia and raising a family, Norm Christie says that Rudolph Cochius returned to Montreal to work on the Stations of the Cross on Mount Royal. While engaged with the project he died of an apparent heart attack in March 1943 at age 65. The man who had done so much to commemorate Newfoundland's war dead was himself gone.

In Que-Que, Tom Nangle was heavily involved with an organization of war veterans called the MOTHs (Memorable Order of Tin Hats). In this organization he did a large amount of community work and made representations to government on behalf of veterans seeking pensions or hospital care. The former padre helped run the local Remembrance Day parade and was the founder and editor of Que-Que's first newspaper. According to his daughter, Mavourneen, he gave all his war pension cheques to needy South African veterans.

In Rhodesia, Nangle maintained his lifelong interest in sports. He helped build a baseball diamond and got a baseball league going. He was also an ardent fisherman. Hugh said his father enjoyed catching and eating fish but wasn't big on hunting. When Hugh considered going into the military as a career, both his parents refused to support the decision:

> *Dad said war was hell for the victors and the defeated, and that it was far too easy to get killed in combat. My mother said that my father understood combat and that I should listen to him.*

His family's life in Rhodesia might have been considered idyllic, said Hugh:

> *The standard of living for the white community was very, very high. Rhodesia never passed apartheid laws like South Africa did, but there was a level of racism. For example, invariably we had a cook and a houseboy. And, there was no integration of blacks and whites in the school system. I went to a government-run, all-white school.*

Hugh said, however, his father felt an integrated education system was necessary and the lack of a proper education system for the African people would eventually cause major problems.

In 1962, Hugh left his home in South Africa and emigrated to Canada to attend university. He eventually married and settled in Toronto. In 1966, on the fiftieth anniversary of the Battle of the Somme, his father attended a reunion and commemoration ceremony at Beaumont Hamel. After that, he and Thelma spent a week in Toronto with Hugh and his wife. They followed with a week in Montreal with Mavourneen and her husband:

> *I had given mother a subscription to MacLean's magazine and she was very interested in coming to Canada. When (Premier) Joey Smallwood learned father was in Canada, he asked him to come to Newfoundland but Dad refused.*

Despite the refusal, Hugh says his father maintained a lifelong interest in what was happening in Newfoundland:

> *If anyone came to Rhodesia from Newfoundland, father tracked them down and got every scrap of information he could about Newfoundland. For example, he didn't think joining Canada was a good thing for Newfoundland. He had a silver caribou that had been presented to him for his work and that was always displayed in our living room in Que-Que. My brother Timothy has it today.*

Tom Nangle read Colonel Nicholson's book *The Fighting Newfoundlander* with great interest. But Hugh said his father thought that Nicholson portrayed him as a "cheerleader" and didn't understand the role of a chaplain. Hugh remembers that July 1st was a very solemn day in the Nangle home when he was growing up in Rhodesia, and after he left:

> *After I left Rhodesia, each year in early July, I would get a letter that Dad had written on July 1st. He would talk about how the Regiment was decimated. He would talk about how Newfoundland was not the first into the line, yet they were pushed on despite the annihilation of the first Regiments to go forward. He said wave after wave of young people were pushed into the line and slaughtered. He used phrases like 'they were thoughtless cannon-fodder.'*

Despite being critical of the way the Royal Newfoundland Regiment was pushed into the firing line on July 1, 1916, Tom Nangle maintained a deep respect for Earl Haig and remained committed to the British Empire.

Hugh and his son, Toby, visited Newfoundland in November 2005, mainly because Toby wanted to see what his grandfather had accomplished in St. John's. On November 11, father and son attended the Remembrance Day ceremonies at the National War Memorial on Water Street. They were pleased to see such a large crowd, and quite proud to think that their father and grandfather respectively had played such a large role in creating the memorial.

As to whether his father ever returned to the Roman Catholic church, Hugh said he has discussed the matter with his sister, who lives in Australia, and they both think their father may have gone back to the church shortly before his death on January 4, 1972.

Thelma died of skin cancer in 1969, three years before Tom. The death of his younger wife was another case of a close personal connection being torn out of Tom Nangle's life. It was sadly ironic that a woman twenty years his junior died before him.

In 1972, the local newspaper in Rhodesia reported Tom Nangle's death:

> *LCol. Thomas Nangle, an old resident of Que-Que died in Shabani Hospital on the 4th January. He was 83. The funeral took place at the Que Que Cemetery at 5 p.m. last Friday, 7th January, and at his own request the service was conducted by the MOTHs Association.*

It seems fitting that Nangle was laid to rest by veterans and comrades from the Memorable Order of Tin Hats because he was a man who spent much time in the military, and did so much to commemorate the sacrifices of common soldiers. But it is sad to think that this native Newfoundlander, who did so much for his country, is buried so far from home.

Young Thomas Nangle (centre sitting), Captian of Championship St. Bon's Cricket Team Circa 1907.

Nangle Family - Rhodesia 1961 (L to R) Hugh, Thelma, Tom, Mavourneen, Timothy, Rory

A storyboard in Beaumont Hamel Memorial Park, France 2006

Commemorating the Battle of Monchy-le-Preux July 2006. (L to R) (The Nangles) Rory, Mavourneen, Gary Browne and Hugh.

Honourary Col. Edward Roberts accompanies the Princess Royal on her inspection of RNR
July 1, 2006, Beaumont Hamel Park

Four Royal Newfoundland Constabulary Officers also members of the RNR at gravesite of Lt. Walter Greene (Newfoundland Constabulary) killed at Battle of Marconing Nov. 20, 1917. (L to R) Const. Jim Lynch, Const. Derek Rumbolt, Const. Alex Brennan, Deputy Chief (Ret.) Gary Browne in rear

~ Chapter Nineteen ~

CONCLUSION

After the Great War ended in 1918, men returned home and went back to their normal lives. There was no counseling, no debriefing, no therapeutic cleansing of the soul and mind. Psychiatry was in its infancy and the term "post-traumatic stress disorder" (PTSD) had not yet been coined. Troubled veterans who were plagued by psychological problems or perhaps alcoholism were said to be "shell-shocked."

In the interest of discussion, the authors felt it was relevant to explore PTSD and its possible impact on Tom Nangle. He lived through the war, saw its horrors and buried his friends, schoolmates and comrades. Then, just months after the war's end, he returned to the battlefields and began the agonizing search for decaying bodies and body parts, and the preparation of organized military cemeteries. Men were disinterred from scattered battlefield graves and if possible identified and re-buried in massive military cemeteries.

What was the possible impact of this awful, but necessary work on Tom Nangle? Was it a factor in his deciding to leave the priesthood and emigrate to Rhodesia? Was he driven to mark the "Trail of the Caribou" by the dead men he buried?

Christie points out in his book: "The war affected the young priest dramatically. The sacrifices of his fellow Newfoundlanders cut him deeply, so much that preserving the memory of 'Ours', as he referred to them, became his life's mission. Sadly the

SOLDIER - PRIEST IN THE KILLING FIELDS OF EUROPE, WW I:

graves of many of those killed or missing were never found. This was a daunting and depressing job." Christie noted that Nangle wrote, "I am afraid the task is hopeless and that very few identifications will be made."

Apparently, to further add to the frustrations, the personal identification discs (dog tags) worn by the British soldiers in World War One were made of fibre rather than of metal, and after burial the dog tag would breakdown and decompose, making identification nearly impossible.

One can only imagine the devastating personal impact upon chaplains in WW1 caused by numerous deaths, and this was especially true for a close homogeneous group like the (Royal) Newfoundland Regiment. This devastation was magnified many times over as a result of the terrible loss of so many young vibrant Newfoundlanders. The following partial list clearly illustrates the tragedy:

Age at Death	Number of Deaths
16	5
17	16
18	48
19	153
20	189
21	191
22	137
23	126
24	107
25	84

Source: *Provincial Archives - MG9 1.02.009 (Captain C.S. Frost Papers)*

These death statistics are clearly reflective of the young soldiers in the Regiment. There are 201 cemeteries where Regiment soldiers of WW1 are buried, and the total number of fatal casualties was 1305 with 591 having no known grave. As

Director of War Graves, Registration, Enquiries, and Memorials, Padre Nangle knew these statistics only too well and they must have scarred him to his soul (source: Prov Archives-MG9 1.02.009)

To better understand PTSD and its possible impacts on Tom Nangle, the authors spoke with Dr. Thomas Cantwell, Clinical Chief of Psychiatric Services for Newfoundland's Eastern Health Board. Cantwell has first-hand experience with PTSD because he counseled several WWII veterans who suffered from it.

"Post-traumatic stress disorder has been there as long as people have been around but it has changed its name many times. In the aftermath of the First World War, people talked about some vets as being shell-shocked," said Cantwell.

By the end of World War One, the Army had dealt with 80,000 cases of shell shock. As early as 1917, it was recognized that war neuroses accounted for one-seventh of all personnel discharged for disabilities from the British Army. "Symptoms ranged from uncontrollable diarrhoea to unrelenting anxiety. Stomach cramps seized men who knifed their foes in the abdomen. Snipers lost their sight. Terrifying nightmares of being unable to withdraw bayonets from enemies' bodies persisted long after the slaughter. Everyone had a breaking point: weak or strong, courageous or cowardly - war frightened everyone witless..." (Professor Joanna Bourke, Birkbeck College for BBC History www.bbc.co.uk/history/).

During our research we found an example where a young soldier of the Royal Newfoundland Regiment, who was lucky enough to survive the Battle of Beaumont Hamel with gun shot wounds to his legs, suffered from major sleeplessness, and other shell shock symptoms. He was hospitalized and initially diagnosed as suffering from alcoholism. This mis-diagnosis was quickly picked up by a very observant British military doctor who said the man was suffering from 'shell shock,' today referred to as Post-Traumatic Stress Syndrome (PTSD).

Cantwell says that we can only begin to try and imagine what life was like in the trenches and on the battlefield. Soldiers lived from "minute to minute and hour to hour." People like Tom Nangle would have had the physical event of friends being killed, but would not have had the time to feel the event on an emotional level and grieve the loss, as should naturally occur. This could easily have resulted in the suppression of strong feelings that would be dealt with openly in the normal course of events.

"I counseled a number of World War Two vets with PTSD. In one case the man was a workaholic his whole life. He was fine until old age slowed him down and then he began to have a flood of memories of the war and what he had seen," said Cantwell. He also explained that workaholism, addictions, broken marriages, suicide, depression and anxiety are all fairly commonly associated with PTSD.

In terms of Tom Nangle's decision to leave the priesthood, we see that when his work was completed with the unveiling of Beaumont Hamel Park in 1925 he soon after decided to leave the church and settle in Africa. Are the events related? Tom Cantwell: "Something motivated this man to go in the priesthood in the first place, and something motivated him to leave. We can't limit it all to his war-time experience, but to have been a counselor or confidant to that group of people (soldiers in the trenches) must have been very confusing. And, he would have seen what appeared to be senseless deaths. It could have had a major impact on his own belief system."

Cantwell speculates that for a priest to serve in a battle setting where one day he was hearing a soldier's hopes, fears and worries, and the next day perhaps burying that man must have had a huge personal cost for Nangle. It would almost certainly have lead to a questioning of one's faith and could have helped motivate him to go to a country like Africa where he could continue his good work.

While Cantwell emphasizes that his analysis is speculative, since Nangle is dead, and is based solely on letters, papers, and interviews his comments do seem to shed some light on Nangle's personality, approach, drive and decision to leave the priesthood and move to Rhodesia.

Why Has Tom Nangle Been Overlooked?

Nangle did a tremendous amount of work for his country and comrades. Yet to date he has been largely overlooked in Newfoundland history. Why is this so?

While we were writing this book many people asked what we were writing about. When we answered, "Father Tom Nangle," the typical response was, "Who was he?"

When asked why he thinks his father has been largely overlooked in Newfoundland history, Hugh Nangle says there a couple of possible reasons. "First was his departure from the priesthood. There was a wiping of the slate, he sort of disappeared. Secondly, he didn't really stay in touch with anyone in Newfoundland. He made a complete and clean break."

Is the fact that Tom Nangle left the priesthood and settled far from Newfoundland part of the reason why he has been largely overlooked in Newfoundland history? We know that Nangle refused Premier Smallwood's invitation to return to Newfoundland in 1966. But years earlier, Governor Harris had declined to follow Prime Minister's Squires recommendation that Nangle be awarded the prestigious C.M.G. For whatever reasons, Harris felt that Nangle did not deserve the honour and so overlooked his extraordinary work.

Nangle's closest ally seemed to have been Governor Davidson, who left Newfoundland in late 1917 and died in Australia in 1923. Other close allies were Sir Richard Squires and Sir William Coaker, Minister of Fisheries in Squires' Administration of 1919 - 1923. Squires was plagued by scandal in 1923 and again in 1932. Perhaps Nangle's association with Squires did him more harm than good.

Another factor that may have played a role in Tom Nangle's being overlooked in Newfoundland history has to do with the suspension of Responsible Government and subsequent Confederation with Canada in 1949.

Still another reason why Tom Nangle may have been forgotten was his "shoot from the hip" attitude. He said what he thought and challenged the dominant ideas of his day. He was not afraid to take sides in a debate. He spoke out publicly against using an educational building as a war memorial. He expressed his opinions however unpopular they might have been.

But given all that he accomplished it is remarkable that no one has given him the recognition he deserves, or at least erected a plaque near the National War Memorial in his memory. As this is the society from which he sprang, we strongly believe that more steps need to be taken to commemorate the work he did.

We are of the firm opinion that Padre Nangle deserved more significant recognition for his war time service to the soldiers of the Regiment, their families and to Newfoundland. It is beyond our understanding how this man was overlooked so many times by his country, province and the military establishment he so proudly and effectively served.

We were thoroughly disappointed to recently learn that the Historic Sites and Monuments Board of Canada rejected a comprehensive submission from Mr. John O'Mara and others asking that Nangle be officially designated a 'person of national significance" and be duly commemorated as such.

Historic Sites and Monuments Board report 2004 - 68 [Alexandra Mosquin] recommended erecting a plaque to Nangle either in Bowring Park near the caribou statue, or at Harborside Park across from the National War Memorial. Sadly, the first time this motion was presented in Ottawa in 2005 it was dismissed because it was deemed "Nangle was not a person of national significance."

We can only speculate that Nangle was overlooked nationally because his accomplishment occurred at a time when we were not part of Canada. He raised monuments for the fallen of the Dominion of Newfoundland, not the Dominion of Canada. The Royal Newfoundland Regiment fought alongside soldiers of sister Dominions such as Australia, South Africa and Canada. Newfoundland had Beaumont Hamel, Canada had Vimy Ridge.

Today, for Canadians to recognize Tom Nangle's important and significant contributions is to remember a time when Newfoundland was a Dominion, not a province.

On February 27, 2006, co-author Gary Browne wrote the Mayor of St. John's, His Worship Andy Wells, and made the case for naming a street after Padre Nangle. At this time, the authors wish to officially recognize the foresight and progressive thinking of the City of St. John's Municipal Council through the personal efforts of Mayor Wells, Deputy Mayor Dennis O'Keefe and the City's Nomenclature Committee for agreeing to the street name - Padre Nangle Place. We sincerely hope this very positive recognition of Newfoundland's soldier-priest by our capital city will prompt others into giving this unsung hero his proper place in our history.

Newfoundland's Loss

Since we are speculating about why Tom Nangle may have left the priesthood and moved to Africa, it is also interesting to consider what he might have accomplished had he chosen to remain in Newfoundland.

What if he had become involved in Newfoundland politics? He was generally well liked and very well respected as a man who got things done. He was politically connected to the upper echelons of Newfoundland society, and he was a powerful orator.

There was talk of the war veterans forming a non-sectarian political party. Imagine if Nangle had created and led such a party. With the support of war veterans throughout the country he may have had a strong power base.

Or what if he had allied himself with another "old soldier," Major Peter Cashin, the man who helped bring down the Squires' Administration in 1932, and was Joseph Smallwood's main anti-Confederate opponent during the National Convention.

What if the team of Nangle and Cashin had worked together? Perhaps Nangle could have pulled more anti-Confederate votes from veterans in the outports. He may have been able to out-duel Smallwood.

All this is pure speculation, but we feel sure that had Tom Nangle remained in Newfoundland, whether as a priest or not, he would have continued to make a major impact on his native land, society and politics. Newfoundland's loss was Rhodesia's gain!

Appendix - A

The Chaplain
[A tribute to Padre Nangle]
By Dan Carroll, in The Newfoundland Quarterly August 1916.

Now in the hour of sacrifice and prayer -
The youthful Priest, the comrade of the corps
The clean Oblation meekly offers there
To God that he may on our soldiers pour
The gifts of courage, fortitude and o'er
Their arms in battle stretch his sheltering hand
Till peace of nations once again restore
Them to the homes and hearts of Newfoundland -
Yet, Father of the World, we bow to Thy command.

Since then the gallant band that worshiped there
Have known the fiery demon of the war,
At Suvla and at Beaumont Hamel, where
There valiant deeds have spread their fame afar
Their actions proved to all whose sons they are
And brought renown unto their native land
Whose heart is constant as the North's true star
However, the storm prevails, steadfast to stand
Till liege to the sea the Belgian arms command.

And now the priest who in that Sabbath hour
Offered the Sacrifice of Calvary
Unto the God of Peace, of war, of Power,
For patience born of strength, till victory
Would crown the soldiers of humanity
has donned the khaki and with heart aglow
to do the patriot's part heroically
o'er field of France he moves to meet the foe
When wounded hearts and souls his shining hand
shall know.

SOLDIER - PRIEST IN THE KILLING FIELDS OF EUROPE, WW I:

There's many a charge and many a halt to be
Ere yet the days of slaughter will have ceased
And many a scene shall need the charity
And the kind office of the comrade Priest
In the assault his voice is not the least
To nerve the soldier, but when death is near
Then is his zeal with God-like love increased
Then are his words of comfort and cheer -
The Church's living voice unto the soldier's ear.

Appendix - B

Father Tom
By James Murphy
October 1917
[Written around the time of Nangle's recruiting lecture
at the Casino Theater in St. John's.]

Oh! Soggarth Aroon, to the dear land that bore you,
We welcome your presence today with great joy;
The blue sky is smiling, the breeze passes o'er you,
The same as you knew them since you were a boy.
The hills which you rambled, the meadows you gamboled
They all seem to welcome you back from the Somme;
The love of the masses, of all creeds and classes
Today goes out to our own "Father Tom."

To all you are welcome for you are from Flanders
Where Our Boys are harnessed to Liberty's car
For true are the hearts of the brave Newfoundlanders
And they are renowned for their deeds in the war
They're brave and they're clever, God keep them so ever
No dread have "Our Boys" of a cannon or bomb
And with them you're blended, of them you've attended
All have a kind word for their own "Father Tom."

Your heart never turned on a creed or a faction
For where you were needed you'll appear
You were seen 'among "Our Boys" in the thick of the action
And that's what the Master picked out for you here.
Our hearts are rejoicing, our tongues are all voicing
The love that we bear you we'll show since you come;
Those friendly old faces, you'll find in their places
To tender a welcome to you "Father Tom."

APPENDIX - C

A memorial plaque was erected at Beaumont Hamel in 1925. In an article written by LCol. Nangle in *The Veteran* magazine (May 1926) the inscription was stated as reading as follows:

A.M.D.G.
NEWFOUNDLAND
WAR MEMORIAL PARK
BEAUMONT HAMEL

THIS PARK EMBRACES THE GROUND OVER WHICH THE NEWFOUNDLANDERS FOUGHT ON THE FIRST OF JULY 1916, AND WAS PURCHASED AND CONSTRUCTED UNDER THE DIRECTION OF

LT. COL. T. NANGLE
and
R.H.K.COCHIUS, ESQ.
Landscape Architect

FROM FUNDS SUBSCRIBED BY THE GOVERNMENT AND WOMEN OF NEWFOUNDLAND AND WAS OPENED BY

FIELD MARSHAL EARL HAIG, K.T.G, G.C.B., O.M.
LATE COMMANDER IN CHIEF OF THE BRITISH EXPEDITIONARY FORCE ON JUNE SEVENTH, 1925.

APPENDIX D

War Related Recognition for Members of The Royal Newfoundland Regiment WW1:

The following is a list of war related recognition for members of the Royal Newfoundland Regiment :

- 1 - Victoria Cross (V.C.);
- 2 - Companion of The Order of St. Michael and St. George (C.M.G.);
- 3 - Commander of The Order of The British Empire (C.B.E.);
- 3 - Distinguished Service Order (D.S.O.);
- 8 - Officer of The Order of The British Empire (O.B.E.);
- 9 - Member of The Order of The British Empire (M.B.E.);
- 1 - Royal Victorian Order (R.V.O.);
- 30 - Military Cross (M.C.);
- 6 - Bar to Military Cross (M.C.& Bar.);
- 31 - Distinguished Conduct Medal (D.C.M.);
- 1 - Bar to Distinguished Conduct Medal (D.C.M.&Bar.);
- 108 - Military Medal (M.M);
- 8 - Bar to Military Medal (M.M. & Bar.);
- 17 - Meritorious Service Medal (M.S.M.);
- 25 - Mentioned in Dispatches;
- 10 - Honourable Mention to Secretary of State for War;

Foreign Awards:

French

- 4 - Croix de Guerre
- 1 - Croix de Guerre avec Etoile d'Or;
- 1 - Croix de Guerre avec Etoile d'Argent;
- 3 - Croix de Geurre avec Etoile de Bronze;
- 1 - Medaille d'Honneur avec Glaives en Bronze;

Belgian

1 - Chevalier de l'Ordre de Leopold II;
8 - Croix de Guerre;

Italian

1 - Cavalier of The Order of The Crown of Italy;
1 - Italian bronze Medal;

Russian

1 - Medal of St. George

There were a total of three General Service Medals that members of The Royal Newfoundland Regiment were eligible to receive during World War One as a part of The British Army:

- The 1914 & 1914-15 Stars;
- The British War Medal;
- The Victory Medal;

The 1914 Star was awarded for service on the establishment of a unit in France or Belgium between August 5 and midnight on November 22/23, 1914. A Bar was awarded to recipients of the Star who served under fire during the respective time.

The 1914-15 Star is identical to the 1914 Star except it is titled 1914-15 rather than Aug-1914-Nov.

The British War Medal (Army) was awarded for service upon entry into a theatre of war on duty, or who left places of residence and rendered approved overseas service between August 5, 1914 and November 11, 1918.

The Victory Medal was awarded to those who served on the establishment of a unit in a theatre of war 1914-18.

[To the best of our combined knowledge LCol. Nangle received the British War Medal and The Victory Medal.]

APPENDIX E

Shortly after the tragic news of Lieutenant Walter Greene's death (November 20, 1917) reached his widowed mother at Bell Island, Newfoundland, his young sister, Rose (Regan), penned a beautiful but sad poem in honour of her brother.

The Soldier

A right brave smile, and a hand clasp true,
A smothered sigh as he bade adieu,
And the soldier lad with martial stride
Is off to the blood and battle tide.
The hopes that are steeped in that soul, who knows
As he wields his might 'against his country's foes.

We look the last into his eyes of truth,
We speak of pride of his strength and youth,
And we deem him fitted for duty's needs,
To help his king for his country bleeds.
Our hearts go out as we say good-bye,
For we know in the strife he will win or die.

Can aught of life's gems bedeck a woe?
Can sorrow be hidden by fame's bright glow?
The eyes that shown bright when the summons came
Are lifeless and cold in his country's name.
That heart beat high at the bugle sound,
Ah! brave were the hopes with which life was bound.

But a smile is wreathing the lips of clay,
A right brave smile, for at break of day
Our soldier went home with his mission done,
And answered the roll call at setting sun.
For his God and his king he has done his part,
And for victory was stamped on his noble heart.

APPENDIX F

Other Chaplains of The Regiment

To the best of our knowledge, there were three other chaplains of the Regiment who served our soldiers in World War One and they are:

Rev. Wilfred Down Stenlake
Rev. Arthur C. Clayton
Rev. G.H. Maidment

Colonel Nicholson in *"The Fighting Newfoundlander"* addresses the problem of no padres being appointed to the Regiment in its early days :

"It was not feasible to provide a chaplain for each denomination, and so none was appointed. The Fist Five Hundred sailed from St. John's without a padre. But the battalion was fortunate in having one of its members, Private W. D. Stenlake, a Methodist student for the ministry, who on the out break of war had left his mission field at Twillingate, Newfoundland to become one of the First Five Hundred. Wilfred Stenlake, a quite, unassuming man, carried on his regular duties as a member of "B" Company, but he was always ready, when a chaplain from brigade headquarters was not available, to read the burial service over a fallen comrade, or - ....- to lead his fellow soldiers in simple but sincere worship and prayer..."

Wilfred Stenlake, originally of the Channel Islands, England, served as a private in Gallipoli where he was infected with a severe case of dysentery which caused him to be invalided to England on January 3,1916 and to be eventually sent back to Newfoundland and medically discharged for being unfit for duty on September 12,1916.He was ordained a full minister of the Methodist Church in February of 1917 at Grand Falls. He applied to the Regiment again in 1917, but this time as a full time padre with the Army Chaplain's Department. Padre

Stenlake received his commission as a chaplain on June 14, 1917. He went on to serve as chaplain with the Army Chaplain's Department in France from July to November 1917, and with the West Indies Regiment, Egyptian Expeditionary Force from June 1918 until July of 1919. Returned to Newfoundland on September 18, 1919, retired on October 14, 1919, and eventually moved to the Wesleyan Theological College Montreal in 1920.

Arthur C. Clayton was a thirty six year old Church of England minister from St. John's when he joined the Newfoundland Regiment in March, was commissioned as a chaplain with the Army Chaplain's Department on April 11, 1916, and was attached to the 26th Division, Etaples, France. Padre Clayton served with the American, Australian and Canadian medical units. From October 1916 until March of 1917 he was attached to the Newfoundland Regiment on the Somme. He passed through gas attacks at Combles, France, and was invalided to Wandsworth General Hospital, England. In May of 1917 returned to Newfoundland and served with Base Depot until peace was declared. He returned to St. Thomas' Church in St. John's where he served as curate.

The Reverend G.H. Maidment of the Church of England joined the Regiment in June of 1917 and went overseas with the Army Chaplains Department where he served for approximately fourteen months. During that period he administered to the Newfoundland and Essex Regiments at the Western Front. On August 18, 1918, Padre Maidment relinquished his commission with the Chaplain's Department and was repatriated to Newfoundland. He returned to Bonne Bay, Newfoundland and continued his ministry. His Regimental records showed that his British War Medal was forwarded to him at Bonne Bay in 1919.

APPENDIX G

Others who assisted Padre Nangle:

Others, to the best of our knowledge, who assisted Padre Nangle after the war as part of the War Graves, Registration and Enquiries Directorate were :

James Lambert, an accountant by profession, enlisted in the Regiment on September 7,1914 and subsequently fought at Gallipoli, and at Beaumont Hamel where he was wounded on July 1, 1916. Later served in the depot at Ayr, Scotland and in the Pay and Records Office in London, England. Discharged on June 1, 1920 . At the request of Padre Nangle he re-enlisted on November 6, 1920, and was later promoted to acting Staff Sergeant Major on special duty with the War Graves, Registration and Enquiries Directorate.

John Cummings, a Methodist school teacher from St. John's, enlisted in the Regiment on August 31, 1915 and was wounded at both Gallipoli and France. In 1921, he was promoted to Acting Staff Quartermaster Sergeant while doing special duty with Padre Nangle on the War Graves, Registration and Enquiries Directorate. He was demobilized back to Newfoundland on June 1, 1921. Padre Nangle referred to Cummings as a " first rate clerk."

John Lawrence Murphy of St. John's joined the Regiment on December 1, 1914 and was wounded in Gallipoli and Monchy, France. Murphy was transferred to the Newfoundland Contingent Office in London, England and in February of 1920 was attached to the War Graves, Registration and Enquiries Directorate to assist Padre Nangle .He was also promoted in 1921 to Acting Staff Sergeant Quartermaster. Murphy was approved for war disability pension on April 1, 1924.

As stated in this book, a telegram was sent to the Prime Minister of Newfoundland on November 1, 1921 from London, England, stating that " Nangle has asked me to recommend following his staff for O.B.E.[Officer of The Order of The British Empire] - James Lambert, John Lawrence Murphy, William Brown." Apparently, Padre Nangle firmly believed the said members of his staff went above and beyond the call of duty while on special duty with the War Graves, Registration, and Enquiries Directorate.

Private Henry Snow of St. John's enlisted in the Regiment on December 28, 1916 and served until the end of the war. He received the Military Medal for conspicuous bravery under heavy machine gun fire, as a stretcher-bearer in attending to the wounded. He was re-attested into the Regiment on July 21, 1919 on special duty to the War Graves, Registration and Enquiries Directorate. Private Snow, who was a stretcher-bearer for a considerable amount of time, would have had much needed knowledge of where soldiers died, and this would have been of valuable assistance to Padre Nangle in grave identification.

APPENDIX H
Chronology of Beaumont-Hamel Managers

In September of 1924 the Newfoundland Government agreed to assume responsibility for expenses related to Beaumont-Hamel Park which included caretaker and lighting of site duties.

Mr. William (Bill) Brown - Mr. Brown, a native of Grimsby, England was caretaker of the memorial from 1924 until the outbreak of the Second World War at which time he returned to England. Following the end of the war he returned to Beaumont-Hamel and assumed his duties until his death in 1954.

During the period from Mr. Brown's death until 1959, there was no on site management of the Memorial. Direction was provided by Col. Allan Chambers in London and Mr. Paul Piroson at the Canadian National Vimy Memorial.

Mr. Paul Addison - Mr. Addison succeeded Mr. Brown and became manager of the Memorial from 1959 to 1964.

Mr. Stephen Austin (Sr) - Mr. Austin assumed his responsibilities as manager on July 1, 1965. He remained un this position until June 30, 1992, with the exception of a brief period in the late 70's when he worked at the Department of Veterans Affairs Office in St. John's.

Mr. Anthony Cooke - Mr. Cooke was manager from August 29, 1979 to December 20th, 1979.

Mr. Vic Snow - Mr Snow was manager from May 20, 1980 to Nov. 14, 1980. Prior to going to Beaumont-Hamel, Mr. Snow worked at the Veterans Affairs office in St. John's.

Stephen Austin (Jr) - Mr Austin, succeeded his father, Stephen Sr., and assumed his duties as manager of the memorial on July 1, 1992, where he remained until March 2000, at which time he transferred to Veterans Affairs Canada's Head Office in Charlottetown, PEI. Mr. Austin currently works as a Senior Program Officer with National and International Memorials, Canada Remembers Division.

Ms. Arlene King - Ms. King is the current manager of the Beaumont-Hamel Memorial and assumed her responsibilities as manager on February 20, 2001. Prior to becoming manager, she came from Parks Canada, where she had held various positions including that of Superintendent, National Historic Sires, Coastal B.C. Field Unit. In this capacity she was responsible for Fort Langley, Fort Rodd Hill and the Gulf of Georgia Cannery National Historic Sites.

National War Memorial: St. John's.

During our research we came upon correspondences from the Governor and the Minister of Public Works offices in relation to the caretaker's position in the mid and late 1920s. August 1927: Governor authorizes caretaker Mr. P, Murphy to perform his duties in uniform.

November 1927: Minister of Public Works advises the National Memorial Committee that his office will continue to pay the caretaker through their committee.

October 12, 1928: Correspondence from the Department of Public Works stating "The caretaker is an ex-serviceman named Mr. P. Murphy."

1928: A number of invoices related to the National War Memorial showing caretaker Mr. Murphy was being paid 75 cents a day in early April and this was upgraded to $1.00 a day from April 19, 1928

References

Cashin, Peter. Major Peter Cashin: My Life and Times, 1890 - 1919. (Edited by Richard Beuhler) Breakwater Books: St. John's 1976

Christie, Norm. For King and Empire: The Newfoundlanders in the Great War, 1916 - 1918.. CEF Books: Ottawa 2003.

Cramm, Richard. The First Five Hundred. C.F.Williams and Son: New York.

Cuff, Robert H. Dictionary of Newfoundland Biography. "Squires, Richard Anderson," pages 323 - 326 Harry Cuff Publications: St. John's. 1990.

Dictionary of Newfoundland and Labrador Biography. Harry Cuff: St. John's.1990.

Dohey, Larry. The Roman Catholic Church in Newfoundland and WWI. Unpublished paper in the Roman Catholic Archives of the Archdiocese of St. John's.1996.

Encyclopedia of Newfoundland and Labrador. Harry Cuff: St. John's. 1993.

Galgay, Frank and Michael McCarthy. Olde St. John's: Stories from a Seaport City. Flanker Press: St. John's. 2001.

Gallishaw, John. Trenching at Gallipoli: A Newfoundland Soldier's Story of the First World War. DRC Publishing. St. John's.2005. (2nd edition) Originally published 1916

Hagerty, James. Benedictine Military Chaplains in the First World War. Paper contained in English Benedictine Congregation History Symposium on internet. 1998.

Kenney, Paul and Tony Murphy. The Trail of the Caribou.

Creative Books: St. John's. 1991.

Lind, Francis T. The Letters of Mayo Lind: Newfoundland's Unofficial War Correspondent, 1914 - 1916. Killick Press: St. John's. 2001. (2nd edition) Originally published in 1919

Military Records of Lieutenant Colonel Thomas Nangle. Provincial Archives of Newfoundland and Labrador.

Minutes of the War Memorial Committee. Provincial Archives. H. Winter Collection. June 1921 - June 1922.

Mosquin, Alexandra. Historic Sites and Monuments Board of Canada Report 2004 (68) on Thomas Nangle.

Nemec, Thomas F. "Postage Stamps" Pages 412 - 425 in The Encyclopedia of Newfoundland Volume 4. 1993. Harry Cuff Publications: St. John's.

Newfoundland Quarterly. Various issues in the Center for Newfoundland Studies, QE II Library, Memorial University of Newfoundland.

Nicholson, Colonel G. The Fighting Newfoundlander: A History of the Royal Newfoundland Regiment Government of Newfoundland.1964

O'Flaherty, Patrick. Lost Country: The Rise and Fall of Newfoundland, 1843 - 1933. Long Beach Press. St. John's.2005

O'Neill, Paul. The Oldest City: The Story of St. John's, Newfoundland Boulder Publications: St. John's. 2003

Records of St. Bonaventure's College in possession of Father Vernon Boyd and Brother J.B. Darcy, Mount St. Francis, St. John's.

Records of the Roman Catholic Archdiocese of St. John's in the Basilica of St. John the Baptist.

Smallwood, Joseph Roberts. "Nangle, Lieut. Colonel Thomas F., page 595 in The Book of Newfoundland Volume 5. Newfoundland Book Publishers: St. John's. 1967

Stacey, A.J. and Jean Edwards Stacey. Memoirs of a Blue Puttee: The Newfoundland Regiment in World War One, DRC Publishing. St. John's. 2002.

The Veteran Magazine. Various issues in the Center for Newfoundland Studies, QE II Library, Memorial University of Newfoundland.

About the Authors

Garrett (Gary) F. Browne, M.O.M.

is Chairman of the Royal Newfoundland Regiment Advisory Council. He is also Deputy Chief of Police (Retired), Royal Newfoundland Constabulary [31 years]. Gary was inducted into the Canadian National Police Order of Merit (M.O.M.) at Rideau Hall in 2001 and became the first Newfoundlander to receive the prestigious honour.

Gary has a long link with the military. He is a former member of the Canadian Armed Forces (Regular) - Royal Canadian Artillery [1966-1969] and is also Past Vice-President Royal Canadian Legion Branch 47, Labrador City. He is also Past President of the Newfoundland and Labrador Army Cadet League and a long time Director with The Signal Hill Tattoo Association.

Gary and his wife of over thirty years, Paula are avid hikers and they have three children - Chris (Pam), Danielle (Steve), and Greg.

Darrin M. McGrath

is a free-lance writer and the author of six books. Darrin has written for national magazines such as Outdoor Canada, Canadian Wildlife, Canadian Geographic, Explore, DownHome Life and Eastern Woods and Waters. He is a contributing editor with The Navigator magazine and is a columnist with the Halifax Herald newspaper.

Darrin is an avid outdoorsman and lives in St. John's with his wife Ann and their five dogs.